MW00446931

HIGHLY-ACCLAIMED CHEF RESTAURATEUR CORY VITIELLO CAN COOK IN A PROFESSIONAL KITCHEN WITH HIS EYES CLOSED (PLEASE DON'T TRY THIS YOURSELF).

However, when he became a dad, he quickly had to adjust his culinary repertoire to cater to a much more demanding clientele: his young family. Now he's ready to share his tips and tricks to turn the dad in your life into a hero in the kitchen.

In his first book, Cory has teamed up with fellow dad and celebrated food writer Chris Johns on a crowd-pleasing collection of recipes that will instill confidence in all home cooks and develop the next generation of adventurous eaters in your family. With Cory and Chris as your guides, you'll find ideas for any time of day, and any day of the week, such as:

- Quick breakfasts to get everyone out the door on time, like Yogurt Oatmeal Pancakes or a Zucchini Omelet with Gouda;

- Light, yet satisfying lunches, like Cory's famous Flock Soba Noodle Bowl or Hot-Smoked Trout & Summer Vegetable Salad;

- Go-to healthy weeknight dinners, like One-Pot Braised Turkey Meatballs or Little Pasta with Swiss Chard & Lentils;

- Weekend projects, like Shaved Brussels Sprouts & Leek Pizza or Cinnamon Buttermilk Ice Cream;

- And, a whole chapter dedicated to every dad's favorite appliance, the barbecue, so he can finally earn that "pitmaster" apron.

With recipes to catapult the cook firmly into superstardom, *Dad in the Kitchen* is a must-have cookbook written by dads *for* dads, but it's also for anyone who might become a dad, or anyone with a dad. And, in the selfless eating-the-crusts tradition of dads everywhere, know that moms, daughters, sons, uncles, aunts, and everyone in between is encouraged to cook from its pages, too.

Dads, grab your tongs—let's do this.

DAD IN THE KITCHEN

DAD IN THE KITCHEN

OVER 100 DELICIOUS FAMILY RECIPES YOU'LL LOVE TO MAKE AND THEY'LL LOVE TO EAT

CORY VITIELLO & CHRIS JOHNS

appetite
by RANDOM HOUSE

Copyright © 2023 Cory Vitiello and Chris Johns

All rights reserved. The use of any part of this publication, reproduced, transmitted in any form or by any means electronic, mechanical, photocopying, recording or otherwise, or stored in a retrieval system without the prior written consent of the publisher—or in the case of photocopying or other reprographic copying, license from the Canadian Copyright Licensing Agency—is an infringement of the copyright law.

Appetite by Random House® and colophon are registered trademarks of Penguin Random House LLC.

Library and Archives of Canada Cataloguing in Publication is available upon request.

ISBN: 9780525611752
eBook ISBN: 9780525611769

Cover and book design by Matthew Flute
Photography by Paula Wilson
Prop styling by Oksana Slavutych; Food styling for chapter openers by Heather Shaw;
Model and occasional assistant, Aubrey Wilson
Printed in China

Published in Canada by Appetite by Random House®,
a division of Penguin Random House LLC.
www.penguinrandomhouse.ca

10 9 8 7 6 5 4 3 2 1

appetite
by RANDOM HOUSE | Penguin
Random House
Canada

To Jillian, Harper Grace, and Bowie,
the people I love to cook for the most.
—Chris Johns

To the two cooks I'm most inspired by:
Mom and Martina. And, of course, Barlow.
—Cory Vitiello

CONTENTS

INTRODUCTION

WHAT A TIME IT IS TO BE A DAD.

In the bad old days, people worshiped rock gods, professional athletes, and movie stars. Not anymore. Now there's no one, with the possible exception of billionaire space pirates, cooler than dads.

Dad jokes, once relegated to the gutter of humor, are now the height of comedy. Dad jeans, long mocked for their weird fade and general dumpiness, are now the fashionista's ultimate aspiration. And as for the dad bod? You may not like it, but that is what the ideal male body looks like.

We're not suggesting that being a dad in the early 21st century is without its challenges: global pandemics, unhinged politics, and impending climate disasters are nobody's idea of a cakewalk, but there's still never been a better time to be a dad. Who would you trade with? Caveman dads, just out there smashing bugs and watching half your family get taken out by saber-toothed tigers? Classical-era dads? Sure, the togas were cool, but get on a Nereid's bad side and suddenly Poseidon's got you chaining your daughter to a rock as a sacrifice to a ravenous sea monster. Medieval dads? Hope you like constant berserk violence and never changing your clothes. Industrial revolution dads? Trick question—pretty much everyone during that time was an orphan and worked in a textile mill from the time they were 6 months old anyway, so dads weren't really part of the picture. Eighties dads? Come on, the haircuts alone.

Nope, as far as being a dad goes, this is it.

If there's one area where dads don't fully dominate the zeitgeist, however, it's food. Somewhere along the line, we think all of us, but especially the fellas, were sold a bill of goods. Thousands of years of patriarchal conditioning taught us to believe that cooking was a chore and something that, if it had to be done at all, should be over and done with as quickly as possible. We couldn't disagree more with that outdated notion. The idea that a woman, or anyone else, should do all the shopping, cook all our meals, and constantly clean up after us seems bizarre, antiquated, and, frankly, unappealing.

Besides, cooking is a blast. Hunting down the best ingredients to feed your friends, your partner, your children, and your family healthy, delicious, lovingly prepared food is a gift. That doesn't mean every meal has to be a six-course blowout, but even simple meals assembled in a hurry or put together from leftovers are an opportunity to share pleasure.

Conveying that pleasure was a big inspiration behind writing this book. We wanted to help dads conquer the final frontier, to become culinary heroes as well as ass-kicking, name-taking, general life-conquering Superdads. We also wanted to make a book that recognized the role today's dad plays in the modern household.

Feeding your friends, your partner, your children and your family healthy, delicious, lovingly prepared food is a gift.

Cory and I both come from restaurant backgrounds—Cory as an owner and chef, and me as a critic and itinerant food writer. When we first sat down to discuss the idea of working on a cookbook, to figure out how to best get Cory's food into the hands and mouths of readers, we realized that although we share a deep and abiding love of restaurants, what really excites us is cooking at home.

We could easily have filled a book with the dishes Cory made his name with from his days running the Harbord Room, or his collection of Flock Rotisserie restaurants, or his work with the Cactus Club Cafe test kitchen. We both realized, however, that home cooking was its own unique beast and that there are things cooks can make at home that simply can't be managed in a busy restaurant kitchen, at least not nearly as well. While some of the recipes he's included here have made appearances in one form or another in his restaurants, they were all tweaked and perfected at home, and most of them are pure home cooking. The recipes are all Cory's and the headnotes for the recipes derive from our conversations about food in general and those specific dishes in particular, so you'll hear his voice throughout those.

We're operating under the belief that the modern dad isn't clueless when it comes to food. Our culture is saturated with cooking shows and cooking competitions, and food porn is as ubiquitous as that other kind of porn. Even people who rarely, or even never, cook have an understanding of food and ingredients that previous generations simply didn't have. It is within living memory that fried calamari was considered an exotic specialty item only to be indulged in by the most adventurous of eaters. Your grandparents—unless they were Hawaiian, in which case, lucky you—probably never had poke tuna in their lives. Now there are six poke places within walking distance of my house. My point is, people's food knowledge has expanded exponentially in the past 20 years, and naturally, that includes dads'.

We're confident that you know how to boil water, light a barbecue, and conjure up a decent grilled cheese sandwich, so we're starting with an assumption of baseline understanding. That said, there are recipes in this book that complete novices can accomplish with ease and those that might teach even more practiced cooks a couple of new tricks. Nothing is beyond your average dad, and all of the recipes are well within reach.

Even more than just a list of ingredients and instructions, however, this book aims to give readers the confidence to apply some of the ideas and techniques contained in these recipes and become more capable and confident cooks with whatever they're preparing. Think of these recipes as templates that are designed to give you the skills to accomplish that particular recipe, and then add your own interpretation as you see fit. Cory's designed these recipes to build cooks, not just people who can follow instructions.

While this is first and foremost a book written by dads for dads, it is also for anyone who might one day consider becoming a dad, and anyone with a dad. Of course, in the selfless eating-the-crust-ends-from-the-loaf-of-bread tradition of dads everywhere, moms, daughters, sons, uncles, aunts, and everyone else are welcome and encouraged to cook from its pages as well.

Let's do this.

KIDS IN THE KITCHEN

"NO ONE IS BORN A GREAT COOK, ONE LEARNS BY DOING."
—JULIA CHILD

Where there are dads in the kitchen, there are sure to be kids, and we wanted to share some of our thoughts on how to involve your entire family in the cooking process. Exposing kids to fresh ingredients, and giving them an understanding of where their food comes from and how it's prepared, is its own reward. Taking pleasure in the ritual of gathering and preparing food more than makes up for the occasional dumped bag of flour.

As an added bonus, we find that getting kids involved in meal prep is a great way to get them comfortable with trying new things. That can start with a trip to the grocery store or farmer's market so they have a better understanding of the whole operation. Shucking corn or pinching the stems off green beans are especially good places to start. And, if you've got the space and ability, a garden, no matter how humble, is a wonderful way to build and strengthen those connections.

The joy of watching a child devour and relish something healthy and interesting that you've made is one of life's great pleasures. We're not above taking some pride in the look on a rival dad's face when one of our kids happily tucks into something sophisticated as well. Beyond that sheer satisfaction, however, we want our kids to be adventurous eaters because it makes our lives easier. Of course, even the most food-forward child is going to have preferences and dislikes. Cory and I both believe that exposing kids to new foods, as well as giving them an opportunity to participate in all aspects of the gathering and preparing of food, is the way to build great eaters. At my house there's a rule that you don't have to like something, but you do have to try it: ridiculously spicy foods excepted. I like to remind my daughter of something I learned in Thailand many years ago. When a person there doesn't enjoy a certain kind of food, they don't say, "I don't like this" or "That's gross." They say, "I don't know how to eat that yet." I love that saying.

We strongly believe that there's no reason that we have to dumb down our food to feed our kids.

The recipes Cory has developed here may not look like traditional kid food, and they never sink to the level of trying to hide an ingredient to try and trick kids into eating it. We want our food to look like itself so that our kids can become familiar and comfortable with it, and then graduate to eating it in a variety of preparations. And many of the recipes have a strong interactive component that encourages kids to, in a sense, play with their food. Ultimately, patience and a genuine appreciation for food and cooking are infectious and will lead to sophisticated, adventurous eaters in short order.

HOW TO USE THIS BOOK

KEEP IT SIMPLE

One of the goals of this cookbook is to give you, the reader, just enough detail to set you up for success, without going overboard and telling you when to take a break to wash your hands. But there are a few basic general rules you should know before getting started.

UNLESS OTHERWISE STATED . . .

- Eggs are large.
- Sugar is granulated.
- All salt is kosher, except for finishing salt (we like Maldon). We sometimes call for fine sea salt as well.
- Pepper is freshly cracked black.
- Milk is homogenized, 3.25% whole.
- Butter is salted. Yes, even for baking.
- Sesame seeds are toasted.
- Herbs are fresh, with the leaves picked and torn by hand—not chopped with a knife.
- Juice is freshly squeezed.
- Oil for frying should be neutral-flavored, like vegetable oil. Oil for salad dressing is olive oil. Any finishing oil is extra-virgin olive oil of a higher quality than you would use in the previous two iterations.
- Nuts can be substituted based on what you have at home, or any allergies. Cory tends to put nuts on many of his dishes, but skip that if it doesn't work for you.

FRESH START

"WHAT NICER THING CAN YOU DO FOR SOMEBODY THAN MAKE THEM BREAKFAST?"

—ANTHONY BOURDAIN

Who has time for breakfast? Like you, we're always in a hurry, and on a typical morning we're usually happy if we can manage a fried egg on toast or a quick bowl of yogurt and some fruit. That's the day-to-day reality, but on weekends, on a holiday, or whenever time permits, it's nice to indulge in something a little more special to start the day.

You could go out for brunch, but let's be honest, that's a nightmare. Besides, getting a few of these recipes under your belt will give you results that no dreary hotel buffet, bottomless mimosa tourist trap, or ersatz Belgian waffle emporium can compare to.

A proper breakfast at home is a luxurious and truly civilized thing. Everybody loves it. It's also a great opportunity to get the kids involved and keep them away from the Saturday morning cartoons for a few minutes.

You don't need help figuring out how to throw some cereal and milk in a bowl, so Cory's come up with a few quick and easy things, alongside a few slightly more involved recipes involving some proper cooking, that maybe you hadn't thought of before but that will take your breakfast game to the next level. As an added bonus, breakfast presents us with an opportunity to master one of the most impactful and stylish dishes a cook has in their repertoire: the omelet. There's a famous story about chefs testing out potential new cooks by asking them to prepare this deceptively simple egg dish. The omelet is the ideal cooking test precisely because there's nothing to hide behind—it's all about technique, timing, and personality. We've got a few variations here that will have you whipping up immaculate omelets in no time.

Cory's also included a few recipes that will satisfy that vegan aunt or the celiac nephew who happens to be visiting, and while a lot of these recipes embrace the more indulgent side of breakfast, they include some clever tweaks that prevent them from sliding into complete excess. As much as we splurge out on decadent meals with our kids, it's nice to have something that still gives the experience of having the kind of fun, hedonistic, sweet breakfast they love, while keeping the ingredients really high quality.

BUCKWHEAT CREPES

SERVES 4–6

This recipe keeps in line with how Martina and I like to eat at home. In the mornings, we both gravitate toward these rich, luscious, almost dessert-like breakfasts: waffles, pancakes, and crepes, especially. We often try to find a way to make them slightly healthier, but in a way that doesn't make us feel we're eating birdseed. Sometimes, when using buckwheat or spelt substitutes, dishes can border on this pressed cardboard texture, but these crepes crisp up well, have a great flavor and texture, and take on a beautiful speckled color. I actually prefer these over a straight all-purpose crepe. Kids can participate in whisking the crepe batter or cracking eggs. And in my experience, especially with breakfast, any time kids can help out, they're more likely to eat the dish and eat a lot of it.

1 cup buckwheat flour

¼ cup spelt flour

3 eggs

1½ cups water

1 cup milk

¼ cup vegetable oil

In a medium bowl, whisk to combine all the ingredients until the batter is smooth and there are no lumps. Cover and let rest for 1 hour or in the fridge overnight. If you make this a day ahead, give the batter a good mix before cooking, because the buckwheat flour tends to separate a bit. If the batter is too thick, adjust with an extra splash of milk or water. It should be just thicker than heavy cream.

In a nonstick skillet over medium-high heat, use an oiled or buttered paper towel to lightly grease the pan. Using a ladle, pour ¼ cup of batter into the center of the pan and swirl to spread evenly. Cook for 30 seconds, then flip. Cook for another 10 seconds on the second side, then transfer to a plate. Repeat with the remaining batter.

I like my crepes folded and served warm with maple syrup, plain yogurt, and some berries or your favorite seasonal fruit. If you have any leftovers, spread some peanut butter and honey overtop, roll them up, and cut them in 2-inch pinwheels for the kids to snack on later.

A NOTE ON FLOUR: We use buckwheat in pastries quite a bit. I like the nutty flavor of it, and the health benefits are undeniable. It's also aesthetically preferable to all-purpose flour, as it's got this kind of bluish, speckled hue that I like in my pastries, breads, and waffles. For our family, health benefits are paramount, so whenever we find something that gives us even a slight benefit, we lean toward incorporating that ingredient, especially with these decadent breakfasts.

ZUCCHINI OMELET WITH GOUDA

SERVES 2–4

1 small zucchini

Kosher salt

6 eggs

2 Tbsp heavy cream

2 Tbsp butter, divided

¼ cup crumbled feta

¼ grated Gouda

1 Tbsp finely chopped chives (optional)

Flaky salt

Black pepper, to taste

I love the combination of zucchini and egg and make a lot of dishes with them, especially during the summer, when zucchini is plentiful. My style of omelet is definitely French-inspired: soft, silky, a little gooey in the middle. I'm looking for that smooth, sunny yellow finish on the bottom with absolutely zero browning, so you get that nice glass-like finish on the outside as opposed to the fried look. The key to a great omelet is the pan. Seriously, the best thing to do is just get a great 8-inch nonstick pan and take very good care of it. Clean it with a soft cloth and wrap it in a dish towel to store it. After that, it's just patience and practice. Ultimately, omelets are not as delicate or intimidating as people think, but they are immensely satisfying to cook and eat.

Coarsely grate the zucchini into a medium mixing bowl—this is a great job for kids; even little ones can usually manage grating something as forgiving as zucchini without incident—and toss thoroughly with ½ tsp kosher salt. Let the zucchini and salt sit for about 15 minutes to pull as much water out as possible.

While that's happening, in a separate bowl, whisk the eggs with the cream until they are just combined with streaks of white still visible. It's important not to mix a lot of air into the egg mixture at this stage.

Using a mesh strainer, press as much moisture out of the zucchini as you can, then transfer it to a clean dish towel. Give it a good squeeze until it is quite dry—kids will love helping with this step. Combine the zucchini with the egg mixture.

In a nonstick pan set over medium heat, heat 1 Tbsp butter until melted and foaming but not browned. Add half of the egg and zucchini mixture and stir gently with a small rubber spatula until the eggs just begin to form a soft, creamy scramble with no liquid running out. Flatten out the eggs using your spatula—they should cover the entire surface of the pan. At this stage, the top surface should look quite raw but not runny.

In a bowl, combine the feta and Gouda. Sprinkle half of the cheese end to end down the horizontal center of the pan. Using your spatula, roll the bottom edge over the cheese center and continue to fold it over on itself like a burrito, closing the omelet with a seal.

Hold the pan directly over the plate and gently turn your omelet out on it, with the seam down. It should be a slim oval shape with no color at all and a clean, slick surface. If it is a little misshaped (and that's okay), use your clean hands to form it into a cigar shape and tuck the edges in.

Garnish with a sprinkle of chives, flaky salt, and pepper.

YOGURT OATMEAL PANCAKES

SERVES 4

½ cup rolled oats, not instant

½ cup + 2 Tbsp milk

1 cup + 2 Tbsp all-purpose flour

1 Tbsp sugar

¾ tsp kosher salt

¾ tsp baking powder

¾ tsp baking soda

1 egg, separated

¼ cup + 1 Tbsp melted butter, cooled

⅓ cup plain, full-fat yogurt

Butter, for frying

For convenience, nothing beats a box of just-add-water pancake mix, but when you want to make pancakes a special-occasion kind of thing, this is the way to go. This recipe, up until the actual cooking stage, is super kid-friendly as well. The oats get an overnight soak in milk, so they have this nice body to them and give an amazing chewy texture to the finished pancake. Whipping the egg whites before incorporating them means the pancakes get a lot fluffier and almost come up like a soufflé. I always send them out one or two at a time as they come out of the pan, so they're fresh as can be. If you've got extra batter, just cook it off and freeze the extra pancakes for a quick toaster snack another day. This is the time to break out the good-quality maple syrup too, and if you can, warm it up a little beforehand for the ultimate breakfast treat.

The night before, in a small bowl, soak the rolled oats in the milk. Set aside in the fridge, covered.

The next morning, in a large bowl, whisk together the flour, sugar, salt, baking powder, and baking soda.

In a small bowl, whisk together the egg yolk, soaked oats, melted butter, and yogurt until well combined.

Pour the yogurt mixture over the flour mixture and stir with a wooden spoon until barely combined, being careful not to overmix. Add the egg white and stir until a thick and somewhat lumpy batter is formed. Set aside for 5 minutes.

Heat a large nonstick skillet over medium heat. Add 1 Tbsp butter, and when it begins to froth, drop about ¼ cup of batter into the pan. You should be able to fit a few pancakes in, but you'll need to cook them in batches. Cook on one side until small bubbles appear on top of the pancake and the sides look dry and airy. Flip and cook on the other side until golden brown, about 4 minutes total. The pancakes can be kept warm in a heatproof dish in a 225°F oven. Serve the pancakes with more butter, seasonal fruit, and maple syrup.

KITCHEN TIP: It is very important not to overmix this batter because the lumps are what give these pancakes their lift, and you don't want to overwork the glutens.

BUCKWHEAT & CHIA WAFFLES

A lot of times I find that gluten-free waffles can be kind of sloppy and anemic in consistency, so I came up with these and made sure to build a lot of crunch into them. Everything stems from the delicate batter that gets loaded up with good things like chia seeds and buckwheat flour. This isn't about trying to fool kids into eating healthy food, though. Everybody loves eating these waffles, it just so happens they're healthy. While this, admittedly, is not exactly a dump-and-stir recipe, if you have 20 minutes on a Sunday morning to make a special batch of waffles, you can feel good about making and eating these.

SERVES 4–6

1 cup buckwheat flour

1 tsp baking powder

1 tsp baking soda

¼ tsp freshly ground nutmeg

½ tsp kosher salt

½ cup ground chia seeds (see tip)

Zest of 1 lemon

3 eggs, separated

1 cup heavy cream

2 cups buttermilk

2 Tbsp maple syrup + extra for serving

2 tsp vanilla extract

In a medium bowl, combine the buckwheat flour, baking powder, baking soda, nutmeg, salt, chia seeds, and lemon zest. Whisk to incorporate, then set aside.

Whip the egg whites with an electric mixer until they reach stiff peaks, about 2 minutes. In a separate bowl, whip the cream to stiff peaks, taking care not to overwhip, about 2 minutes.

In a large bowl, mix the buttermilk, egg yolks, maple syrup, and vanilla until combined. Whisk the dry ingredients into the wet until fully incorporated. Fold in the egg whites, taking care to retain as much air as possible. When the egg whites are almost fully incorporated, fold in the whipped cream.

Preheat your waffle iron. Pour in some batter and cook for about 4 minutes or whatever your appliance suggests. Serve with yogurt, seasonal fruit, and maple syrup.

KITCHEN TIP: You can find ground chia seeds at your local health food store.

AVOCADO TOAST WITH STEAK, PICKLED ONIONS & BLACK SESAME

SERVES 4

4 slices crusty sourdough,
   cut ½ inch thick

2 Tbsp olive oil + extra
   for garnish

1 clove garlic, halved

1 cup Sweet Pea & Avocado
   Guacamole (page 45)

2 radishes, thinly sliced

One 8 oz cooked medium-rare
   steak, trimmed of fat and
   sinew and thinly sliced

Quick Pickled Onions (see below)

1 Persian cucumber, thinly sliced

2 sprigs dill, picked

Kosher salt and black pepper

Black sesame seeds

This is the best thing a person can do with leftover steak, but the real key here is great toast. You want a proper rustic, seeded sourdough, something with a bit of chew to it. Of course, a good, well-smashed avocado is important too. Martina and I use a ton of chili lime salt in our cooking and it goes very well here. While this is a great way to use up leftover steak, it can just as easily be made from scratch. Cook up your preferred cut—striploin, t-bone, ribeye—as you normally would. Just remember to trim it of any connective tissue and thinly slice it against the grain so it's easy to bite through on toast.

Toast the bread on a grill or under the broiler until well browned. Place the bread on a serving platter, drizzle with oil, and rub the toast with the cut side of the garlic clove.

Spread a generous amount of guacamole on the base of each toast, followed by some radish slices, steak slices, pickled onions, cucumber slices, and picked dill. Garnish with an extra drizzle of olive oil and a healthy pinch of salt, pepper, and black sesame seeds.

QUICK PICKLED ONIONS

SERVES 4

½ cup rice wine vinegar

½ Tbsp sugar

1 tsp kosher salt

½ clove garlic

Pinch dried chili flakes

½ small red onion, thinly sliced
   into ½-inch moons

In a small saucepan, boil the vinegar with the sugar, salt, garlic, and chili flakes, then pour over the onions and let sit for 15 minutes. The pickled onions can be made ahead and stored in the fridge for weeks.

BAKED RICE PUDDING

Everybody's childhood is littered with some kind of horrible rice pudding dish, and most people hate it. I get it. If I go to a deli and see rice pudding, I'm always tempted to order it, but it so rarely delivers. The purpose of this recipe is to try to bring rice pudding back into favor, where it belongs. My maternal grandmother always had a version of this rice pudding in her fridge, and she made it in this very particular way, mixing the boiled rice with egg whites and topping it with a generous amount of cinnamon. It was the egg whites that made it different and gave it a nice, light mouthfeel. The one thing I have changed is that after I incorporate the egg whites, I bake the pudding for a bit to give it a soufflé-like quality. That does mean it has to be consumed right away, though, which makes it much more conducive to home cooking than it being a restaurant dish. Personally, I prefer to use a virgin batch of rice; I've always found leftover rice tastes a bit like the fridge, but you could use it in a pinch. I like it my way, but honestly, if you decide to keep it unbaked, it's perfectly good that way too.

SERVES 6

4 eggs, separated

3 cups milk

¾ cup heavy cream

½ cup sugar

¼ cup maple syrup

½ Tbsp vanilla extract

1 tsp cinnamon

⅛ tsp freshly ground nutmeg

⅛ tsp cardamom

3 cups cooked white rice

1 cup raisins or currants

2 Tbsp butter

Preheat the oven to 350°F and butter a 9-inch square casserole dish.

In a large bowl, mix the egg yolks, milk, cream, sugar, maple syrup, vanilla, cinnamon, nutmeg, and cardamom until well combined. Stir in the white rice and raisins until evenly distributed.

Whip the egg whites with an electric mixer on high speed for about 3 minutes, until light and fluffy. Gently fold the whites into the rice mixture.

Transfer the rice pudding to the buttered dish. Dot with the 2 Tbsp butter and place on the middle rack of the preheated oven.

Bake for about 45 minutes, or until the top is golden brown and the custard is set but still jiggly in the center.

THE MEANING
OF LUNCH

"DESTINY MAY RIDE WITH US TODAY, BUT THERE IS NO REASON FOR IT TO INTERFERE WITH LUNCH."

—PETER THE GREAT

Breakfast might be important, but a proper lunch is sublime. Ideally, it involves day drinking and, whenever possible, sunlight-dappled terrazzo courtyards shaded by walnut pergolas, and strong coffee alongside something sweet at the end. It should be a struggle to get up from the chair after a great lunch. You simply cannot have too many meals like that.*

Such a meal is a rare treat, we recognize that, but all the more special because of it. Like most everybody, weeknight meals take up the bulk of our cooking time, but that's no reason we shouldn't aspire to the occasional quality lunch.

Even when it's not a full-blown al fresco showstopper, we sometimes like to make lunch the central meal of the day. Eating like this, especially during the summer or while on vacation, really seems to work well with the rhythms of the day: a quick breakfast, a laid-back, slightly indulgent lunch, and then a glorified snack for dinner.

The following recipes were originally created for just such occasions. Most of them require little heavy lifting and can be thrown together with ease. Almost all of them are, by pure happy coincidence, demonstrably healthy. Some would go best with a picnic blanket and a glass of rosé, while others wouldn't be out of place alongside an ocean view or simply on a backyard patio.

There is, of course, no rule that you have to serve these dishes at lunch, and every one of them works beautifully as either part of a meal or a light dinner on its own.

---

* Your family doctor may disagree.

HOT-SMOKED TROUT & SUMMER VEGETABLE SALAD

This is all about celebrating the sweet ripeness of summer vegetables, most of them raw and fresh, and giving them some heft by introducing rough hunks of hot-smoked trout and serving them with wedges of a crisp potato pancake. The recipe calls for dill, an excellent and underrated herb that deserves its starring role, but feel free to use basil, mint, chives, or a combination of all of them. Little hands tend to do well with the otherwise tedious job of picking the fresh parts of herbs, an activity that helps kids become familiar and comfortable with the different herbs, while improving the dish.

SERVES 4

½ lb green beans, trimmed

½ bunch asparagus, woody ends removed

1 cup mixed cherry tomatoes, halved

1 cup sliced baby cucumbers

½ cup sliced radishes

2 cups packed green leaf lettuce

1 Belgian endive, quartered and core removed

½ cup picked parsley leaves

½ cup picked dill leaves

½ cup Apple, Thyme & Shallot Vinaigrette (page 224), divided

1 side (about 10½ oz) hot-smoked trout, skin removed and broken into large pieces

1 avocado, thinly sliced

4 soft-boiled eggs (5 minutes), cooled and halved

1 Potato Pancake (page 31), cut into wedges

1 green onion, thinly sliced, for garnish

Flaky salt

Black pepper

Bring a large pot of salted water to a boil over high heat, and prepare a large bowl with ice water. Blanch the green beans for 2½ minutes, then transfer to the ice bath to cool. In the same water, blanch the asparagus for 1 minute, until barely tender, then transfer to the ice bath to cool as well. Trim the asparagus into 1-inch pieces and leave the green beans whole.

In a large bowl, toss the green beans, asparagus, cherry tomatoes, cucumbers, radishes, lettuce, endive, picked parsley, picked dill, and three-quarters of the vinaigrette until everything is evenly coated. Place the vegetables on a large serving platter and arrange the trout, avocado, eggs, and potato pancake overtop. Garnish the potato pancake with the green onions. Drizzle the remaining vinaigrette overtop, lightly season with salt and pepper, and serve immediately.

POTATO PANCAKES
SERVES 4

3 medium Yukon Gold potatoes

1 small onion

⅓ cup all-purpose flour

2 eggs, beaten

1½ tsp kosher salt

1 tsp black pepper

½ cup vegetable oil, divided

Preheat the oven to 425°F and place a cast-iron pan inside to heat up.

Fill a medium bowl halfway with cold water. Using the largest hole of a box grater, grate the potatoes into the water—you should get about 4 cups of potatoes. Swirl the water and potatoes around with your fingers to help remove any excess starch—a very child-friendly job. Drain and discard the starchy water.

Grate the onion into the potatoes. Using a clean dish towel or paper towel, wring out any excess moisture from the onions and potatoes, working in batches. This is a very important step in ensuring your potato pancakes are crispy.

Add the flour to the potato mixture. Using a fork, toss the mixture so that every piece of potato and onion is lightly coated. Add the eggs, salt, and pepper and toss until fully incorporated.

Carefully remove the cast-iron pan from the oven and add ¼ cup oil. When the oil starts to shimmer, add half of the potato mixture. Arrange in a thin, even layer over the bottom of the pan. Return the pan to the oven and cook for about 10 minutes, until the bottom begins to crisp and become golden brown. Carefully flip the pancake and cook for 10 minutes, or until golden brown and crispy. Transfer the pancake to a cooling rack or paper towel to drain. Discard the oil remaining in the pan. Add the remaining ¼ cup fresh oil to the pan and repeat with the second half of the potato mixture. Cut the pancake into wedges and serve immediately.

POTATO PANCAKE

HOT-SMOKED TROUT DIP

SERVES 4–6

This is the ultimate summertime picnic dip as far as I'm concerned. Stick it in a deli container with some sliced baguette or a box of soda crackers, grab the bikes, head over to the park, pop a bottle of wine, and it's a picnic. I've been making a version of this dish since my days at Scaramouche, although it's morphed many times over the years. It has a fun '80s retro feel to it. I get a lot of requests for this recipe and it's been shared often. Feel free to pass it along yourself.

½ shallot, minced

Zest and juice of 1 lemon

1 tsp kosher salt

½ tsp black pepper

1 side (about 10½ oz) hot-smoked trout

¾ cup full-fat cream cheese

⅓ cup full-fat sour cream

2 Tbsp finely grated horseradish or 1 Tbsp jarred white horseradish

⅓ cup loosely packed coarsely chopped dill

⅓ cup loosely packed coarsely chopped chives

In a medium bowl, combine the shallots, lemon zest, lemon juice, salt, and pepper. Allow to sit while you prep the remaining ingredients.

Separate the trout from the skin and, using your hands, break up the fish into shreds and set aside. Add the cream cheese, sour cream, horseradish, dill, and chives to the shallot mixture. Mix thoroughly until smooth. Add the trout pieces and stir until just mixed. Serve on crackers or toast or as a dip with vegetables. Any leftover dip will keep for up to 4 days in the fridge.

SHAVED FENNEL & ZUCCHINI SUMMER SALAD

SERVES 4

When you're cooking in the summer, the last thing you want is to be stuck in the kitchen all day, and this is an impressive salad that takes only minutes to put together. The key here is to shave the zucchini wafer-thin, ideally with a mandoline, but if you don't have one or are intimidated by it, with a vegetable peeler. You also want to shave the zucchini at the last possible minute and in elongated pieces rotating around the core, so you're not getting that spongy middle. The long, thin ribbons soak up the flavors of the herbs, olive oil, and lemon.

½ shallot, minced

Kosher salt

1 Tbsp freshly squeezed
   lemon juice

1 Tbsp white wine vinegar

2 small yellow zucchini

2 small green zucchini

1 bulb fennel, quartered
   and core removed

1 cup parsley leaves

1 cup basil leaves

½ cup mint leaves

½ cup dill fronds

2 tsp grainy Dijon mustard

1 tsp honey

Black pepper

½ cup olive oil

¼ cup finely chopped dill

½ long red chili, seeded and
   thinly sliced

½ cup skinned hazelnuts,
   toasted and cracked

1 small wedge ricotta salata

½ lemon, for garnish

In a small bowl, combine the shallots with a pinch of salt, the lemon juice, and the white wine vinegar. Allow this to sit while preparing the remaining ingredients.

With a vegetable peeler, mandoline, or sharp knife, finely shave the zucchini lengthwise into ribbons. Finely shave the fennel, keeping the size as consistent as possible with the zucchini.

In a large bowl, place the zucchini, fennel, parsley, basil, mint, and dill fronds. Toss until well combined.

To the shallot dressing, add the mustard, honey, some pepper, and olive oil and mix until homogeneous. Add the finely chopped dill and mix again.

Add half of the dressing to the salad and toss until everything is evenly coated. Arrange on a serving platter and top with chilies and hazelnuts. Shave the ricotta salata into ribbons overtop, garnish with a squeeze of lemon juice, and serve immediately.

CALI-INSPIRED AVOCADO RANCH SALAD

SERVES 4 AS A SIDE OR 2 AS A MAIN

1 head Boston lettuce, leaves
   washed and separated

2 cups cooked quinoa

½ avocado, sliced

2 radishes, thinly sliced

½ cup halved cherry tomatoes

½ cup sliced Persian cucumbers

¼ cup Quick Pickled Onions
   (page 23; optional)

1 Tbsp black sesame seeds

Buttermilk Avocado Ranch
   (page 225)

¼ cup toasted sunflower seeds

¼ cup crumbled feta

¼ cup sliced chives

Salads like this pretty much defined California spa cuisine for about a decade. The state has established itself as a phenomenal and extremely innovative food destination in its own right, but this kind of fresh, hearty, delicious, and healthy salad still puts me in mind of palm trees and Venice Beach.

On a large platter, place the Boston lettuce leaves, quinoa, and sliced avocado. Arrange the radishes, cherry tomatoes, cucumbers, pickled onions, and black sesame seeds overtop. Add the dressing and garnish with sunflower seeds, feta, chives, and fermented chilies. If you want to make this a complete lunch, add a few soft-boiled eggs on top.

TUNA, AVOCADO, WHITE BEAN, DILL & CELERY SALAD

SERVES 2–4

This is where you want to splash out on a good tin of good-quality tuna. The Spanish and Portuguese stuff is almost always high quality. You could use any old tin from the local supermarket of course, and the salad will still be decent, but quality tuna will make a huge difference. As with any vinaigrette, this one asks you to soak your shallots in the vinegar and lemon juice for a few minutes before adding the rest of the ingredients. It's a small thing that makes a big difference.

1 shallot, thinly sliced

2 Tbsp white wine vinegar

1 Tbsp freshly squeezed lemon juice

¼ cup extra-virgin olive oil

2 Tbsp capers

2 tsp honey

Kosher salt and black pepper, to taste

One 5 oz can good-quality oil-packed tuna, drained

One 15 oz can small white cannellini beans

4 stalks celery, trimmed and thinly sliced

2 Persian cucumbers, thinly sliced

1 cup packed parsley leaves

½ cup packed dill leaves

1 avocado, sliced

Crusty bread, for serving

Fermented Red Chilies, for serving (page 227; optional)

Prepare your dressing by soaking the sliced shallots in the vinegar and lemon juice for 10 minutes. Whisk in the olive oil, capers, honey, salt, and pepper.

In a large bowl, toss together the drained tuna, white beans, celery, cucumbers, parsley, and dill until everything is evenly distributed. Add half the dressing and mix gently to combine. Pile the salad in a serving bowl or on a platter and garnish with sliced avocado and extra dressing drizzled overtop to taste. Serve with good-quality crusty bread and fermented chilies.

ROASTED BEET, KALE & QUINOA BOHO SALAD

SERVES 4

2 large heirloom beets

1 large field carrot

1 head lacinato kale,
   stemmed and thinly sliced

1 cup cooked red or
   white quinoa

1 cup cherry tomatoes

1 red pepper, finely sliced

¼ cup toasted pumpkin seeds

¼ cup pomegranate seeds

¼ cup dried currants

¾ cup Roasted Beet & Citrus
   Dressing (page 223)

This is a take on the most popular salad at Flock, and by publishing it here I'm giving up one of the secret dressing recipes. Think of this as a full meal salad. It's a little time-consuming, but it lasts for a while in the fridge. It's loaded with all kinds of superfood antioxidants and good-for-you ingredients, but don't let that scare you—it tastes great. Our dressings are vegetable-, herb-, and citrus-heavy with just enough good-quality olive oil to emulsify them without adding a whole lot of volume. This allows the flavor of the ingredients to stand out. Massaging the kale with a bit of salt and olive oil until it almost starts to bruise breaks down the fibers and makes it easier to digest.

Preheat the oven to 400°F and line a baking sheet with aluminum foil. Wrap one of the large beets in a second sheet of foil and prick a few times with a fork. Roast for 1 hour, until very tender, then let cool completely. Once cool, peel and slice.

Peel the second beet and shred it on a box grater, using the largest holes. Shred the carrot as well, using the same holes.

In a large salad bowl, lay the kale as the base followed by little piles of shredded beets, shredded carrots, roasted beets, quinoa, cherry tomatoes, red peppers, pumpkin seeds, pomegranate seeds, and currants on top, keeping it all neat and compartmentalized. This gives your family or any picky eaters the chance to pick and choose the toppings they like best. However, if you prefer to toss it all into a slaw, have at it.

Serve with a generous amount of the beet and citrus dressing.

KITCHEN TIP: This is a perfect lunch with a few slices of cold roasted chicken and half an avocado.

SWEET PEA & AVOCADO GUACAMOLE

**SERVES 4 OR
1 HUNGRY CORY**

1 avocado, crushed

1 cup blanched sweet peas, mashed

1 minced jalapeño

1 clove garlic, finely grated

1 green onion, finely sliced

2 Tbsp chopped cilantro

2 tsp kosher salt

2 Tbsp freshly squeezed lime juice

1 Tbsp olive oil

When I have guacamole, I don't want just a little bit—I want to go hard on the stuff. That's part of the reason we developed this recipe at the Harbord Room back in the mid-aughts. In addition to being fairly health-conscious, this version is also a little easier on the pocketbook. Beyond that, though, I like the way the peas take what is traditionally a relatively heavy dish and lighten it up while imbuing it with this vibrant green color. Besides, it makes you feel better when you consume shocking amounts knowing that half of it is peas.

In a medium bowl, combine all the ingredients together and mash until chunky but cohesive. Serve as a dip with chips or crisp vegetables.

ROASTED SWEET POTATOES WITH BUTTERMILK AVOCADO RANCH

SERVES 4

2 sweet potatoes

1 Tbsp olive oil

Kosher salt and black pepper,
  to taste

Pinch chili lime salt, for dusting
  (I like Tajín)

Buttermilk Avocado Ranch
  (page 225)

Think of this as a relatively healthy dish masquerading as something indulgent. The health benefits of sweet potatoes are well known—fiber, vitamins (C and B6 especially), and minerals—but even if they were no healthier than regular russet potatoes, their sweet, creamy flavor and texture would make them a favorite around my house. Sliced into wedges and baked in a hot oven, they take on this nice, caramelized crust that makes a great toasty foil for the creamy avocado ranch.

Preheat the oven to 400°F.

Slice the sweet potatoes into wedges, place in a bowl, and toss with olive oil, salt, and pepper. Arrange the potatoes, skin side down, on a baking sheet and roast for 40–45 minutes, until tender and browned. Dust with the chili lime salt and serve with the avocado ranch on the side.

BRAISED RAPINI & BUFFALO MOZZARELLA FOCACCIA PANINO

SERVES 2–4

1 bunch rapini

3 Tbsp olive oil + extra to taste

1 onion, minced

1 clove garlic, minced

1 tsp kosher salt + extra to taste

½ cup water

¼ tsp chili flakes

8 × 8-inch piece focaccia
  (see note)

1 ball fresh buffalo mozzarella

1 tomato, sliced

½ cup packed basil leaves

Black pepper

Fermented Red Chilies (page 227)

Is it a classic sandwich? I don't know, but this technique of slow-cooking and stewing the rapini is something I use often in different areas. I'll put it on a little crostino in the morning with some white beans and shaved cheese, or even a poached egg; I'll use it on the base of a pizza; I'll use it when I'm making orecchiette. It definitely gets a lot of playtime in our house. The sandwich itself doesn't have a ton of texture—the whole thing produces quite a bit of juice that gets soaked up by the focaccia. For me, this is real home cooking. You could never serve something like this in a restaurant because it wouldn't hold up or taste nearly as good.

Remove the woody ends of the rapini and chop into bite-sized pieces. In a medium saucepan set over medium heat, heat the olive oil. Add the onions, garlic, and 1 tsp salt and cook until fully softened, about 5 minutes. Add the rapini, water, and chili flakes, and cover. Cook for 20 minutes, or until the rapini is cooked through and softened completely. Remove the lid and let the water evaporate.

Slice the focaccia in half horizontally and build a sandwich with rapini, torn mozzarella, tomato slices, and basil. Season with salt, a drizzle of olive oil, pepper, and a generous portion of fermented chilies to taste.

KITCHEN TIP: You can use the pizza dough on page 112 as the focaccia base, or you can buy store-bought—whatever makes your life easier.

CRUSHED CHILLED TOMATO SOUP WITH BURRATA

SERVES 4

This is an old Harbord Room staple that showed up every summer for 10 years. It's a simple preparation that results in a deceptively complex soup. There's a balance between the rustic approach to the tomatoes that you crush by hand and the aromatics that you perfectly brunoise. This is a great opportunity to work on your knife skills and take time to get even, perfectly cut micro-dice on those vegetables. It's good practice and it makes the presentation of this dish really spectacular. However, if there's just too much going on, feel free to take a more rustic approach and casually dice everything up. Heck, if your kids are comfortable with knives, this is the time to simply let them chop away. Finished with some good olive oil, quality balsamic, and toasted sourdough breadcrumbs, this packs a lot of star power at a dinner party.

TOMATOES

2 lb (4–5) very ripe seasonal tomatoes, stems removed and quartered, room temperature

1 Tbsp kosher salt + extra to taste

SOUP

½ cup finely diced (⅛ inch) shallots

3 Tbsp white wine vinegar

½ cup seeded and finely diced (⅛ inch) English cucumbers

½ cup finely diced (⅛ inch) celery

GARNISH

One 7 oz ball burrata

Pinch flaky salt

Splash good-quality extra-virgin olive oil

Splash good-quality balsamic vinegar

½ cup packed basil leaves

Black pepper, to taste

¼ cup Toasted Sourdough Breadcrumbs with Rosemary & Sea Salt (page 228)

In a bowl, macerate the quartered tomatoes in the kosher salt. Mix well with your hands, slightly bruising the tomatoes without pulverizing them. Let stand for 1 hour at room temperature, stirring once halfway through.

In a separate bowl, combine the diced shallots and vinegar and let sit for 30 minutes.

Crush the salted tomatoes with your hands until they are as broken down and pulpy as you can get them. Take a pasta colander (not a fine sieve) and press the tomatoes through using a ladle or simply your hand, making sure to catch the juice, pulp, and seeds in a large bowl. You can also use a food mill, if you have one. We are trying to remove the skins only and retain a lot of the fleshy texture of the tomatoes. Check the crushed tomatoes for seasoning and add a little salt if necessary.

Stir in the diced cucumbers, celery, and vinegar-soaked shallots (along with the vinegar). At this point the soup can be chilled for a few hours or up to the day before, but my preference is to serve it straight away, at room temperature, while the textures and flavors are so alive.

Garnish the soup with a scoop of burrata served cut side up, a pinch of flaky salt overtop, a drizzle of olive oil and balsamic, a scattering of fresh basil, a twist of black pepper, and a crunchy spattering of toasted sourdough breadcrumbs.

BAKED CAULIFLOWER "MAC 'N' CHEESE"

SERVES 4–6

All the cheesy goodness of mac and cheese in a somewhat healthier package. This has always been part of the menu at Flock and it makes a great accompaniment to any kind of barbecue. If you want to make it extra special, once you've combined all the ingredients, put the cauliflower and cheese into little individual cast-iron pans or mini cocottes and give everybody their own. You can't go wrong with cruciferous vegetables and cheese sauce.

1 head cauliflower

½ cup butter

¼ cup all-purpose flour

2½ cups milk

1½ tsp Dijon mustard

2 tsp kosher salt

1 tsp fresh pepper

2½ cups grated cheddar, divided

1 cup grated Parmigiano-Reggiano, divided

½ cup Toasted Sourdough Breadcrumbs with Rosemary & Sea Salt (page 228)

Preheat the oven to 400°F and bring a large pot of well-salted water to a boil.

Break up the cauliflower into small florets and blanch in the boiling water for about 4 minutes (the cauliflower should still have some bite). Set aside to drain well.

In a medium pot set over medium heat, melt the butter. Add the flour and whisk until the flour has been toasted in the butter but hasn't yet begun to brown. Add the milk, whisking constantly, until the mixture is thickened and creamy. Add the mustard, salt, and pepper and whisk to incorporate. Add 2 cups cheddar and ½ cup Parmigiano-Reggiano and stir continuously until the sauce is smooth and creamy. This is a fun sauce to involve the kids in. Let them whisk while the flour toasts and as each ingredient is added so they can watch the sauce come together and thicken up.

Add the drained cauliflower to the sauce and toss to coat. Fold in the remaining ½ cup cheddar. Pour the cauliflower and cheese sauce mixture into a casserole dish. Generously sprinkle with the toasted sourdough breadcrumbs and the remaining ½ cup Parmigiano-Reggiano. Bake in the oven for 30 minutes, until golden brown and bubbly.

FLOCK SOBA NOODLE BOWL

This salad is a power bowl packed full of crunch. You've got this crispy tofu with all the fresh vegetables, and the sweet potatoes act almost like croutons after they're glazed and heavily roasted in the oven until they form a crusty skin. The soba noodles are really healthy: they're made of buckwheat, which is full of manganese and thiamine, so they're low-calorie and gluten-free, but beyond all that, they're a versatile staple to keep in the pantry. They cook up quickly, you can serve them hot or cold, and they work with a wide variety of flavors. This recipe can also carry over well throughout the seasons. It's the perfect summer al fresco bowl, but it's also a nice, bright offering in the winter to liven up your week.

SERVES 4

1 large sweet potato

1 block extra-firm tofu

1 cup Miso, Maple & Citrus Dressing (page 224), divided

8 oz soba noodles

1 bunch spinach

2 cups finely sliced red cabbage

1 cup picked cilantro leaves

1 avocado, sliced

½ cup thinly sliced red radishes

½ cup thinly sliced green onions

½ cup picked basil leaves

1 cup julienned carrots

½ cup edamame

Toasted white and/or black sesame seeds, for garnish

Preheat the oven to 375°F and line a baking sheet with parchment paper. Dice the sweet potato and tofu into ½-inch cubes (or get the kids to do it; tofu cuts super easily and safely). In a medium bowl, toss the sweet potatoes and tofu with 2 Tbsp miso dressing. Spread out evenly on the baking sheet and bake for 30 minutes, or until golden brown, flipping halfway through.

In a pot of lightly salted boiling water, cook the soba noodles, stirring occasionally, for 5–6 minutes, until soft with a slight bite.

Drain and rinse the soba noodles under cold water, running your fingers or tongs through the noodles for 1 minute with the water running to remove excess starch. Fully drain and lightly toss with 1 Tbsp miso dressing to prevent sticking.

Make a base of spinach in a large bowl or platter. Twist a nest of noodles in the middle and arrange your fresh vegetables and herbs around the edge. Top with your hot roasted tofu and sweet potatoes and generously pour your desired amount of miso dressing overtop. Garnish with a liberal sprinkle of sesame seeds.

KITCHEN TIP: Make a double or triple batch of the dressing and keep it at the ready. You can use it for all kinds of things—glazing fish or vegetables or tossed into a coleslaw. It'll last in the fridge for weeks.

HONEY CHICKEN

SERVES 4

The combination of soy sauce, honey, ginger, and garlic is an all-time winner that even the pickiest eaters tend to love. In this recipe, the sauce thickens as it cooks, turning into a dark, burnished glaze over the juicy thighs. Be generous with the green onions, cilantro, and sesame seeds, as they liven up the whole dish—there's no technique here, so just make the garnishes rain. It's a perfect thing for kids to get involved in. Be sure to spoon any extra sauce over the rice.

8 (about 1½ lb) bone-in, skin-on chicken thighs

¾ cup soy sauce

⅓ cup honey

⅓ cup chicken broth or water

2 Tbsp grated ginger

3 cloves garlic, grated

Green onions, finely chopped

Picked cilantro

Sesame seeds

1 sliced long red chili, optional (see note)

Jasmine rice, for serving

Preheat the oven to 400°F.

In a cast-iron pan set over medium-high heat, sear the chicken thighs until golden, about 2 minutes on each side. Remove the chicken, then drain the fat from the pan.

Combine the soy sauce, honey, chicken broth, ginger, and garlic in the skillet and set over low heat, until the honey is melted and the sauce has emulsified.

Arrange the chicken in the skillet, thoroughly coating it with the sauce, and bake for 45 minutes, until the chicken is cooked through and very tender. Baste the chicken a few times during the cooking. Garnish with green onions, cilantro, sesame seeds, and red chilies, and serve with jasmine rice. This dish works well with the Sticky Soy Eggplant on page 92 and the Crushed Cucumber Salad on page 69.

KITCHEN TIP: You can cut the heat of the chili by rinsing it repeatedly under cold water.

TAHINI HONEY COOKIES

MAKES 18 COOKIES

1 cup tahini

⅔ cup honey

1 tsp vanilla extract

½ tsp baking soda

½ tsp kosher salt

2 cups almond flour

⅓ cup white sesame seeds

¼ cup black sesame seeds

I've got an addiction to cookies and ice cream, and there's nothing better to my mind than an ice cream sandwich. In fact, I first made these cookies for an ice cream sandwich because they have a nice chew to them (if you really want to go for it, try them with cinnamon ice cream), but they still taste fantastic on their own. These are delicate and not super sweet, they're a dead-easy freezer cookie, and they highlight the Mediterranean flavors I love so much. The rich honey and tahini are offset beautifully by the delicate shell-like texture from the sesame seeds. This is also a fun dish to make with kids, who love rolling the dough up into ping-pong-sized balls and then flattening them out with the bottom of a mug.

Line a baking sheet with parchment paper.

In a bowl and using a wooden spoon, mix together all the ingredients except the sesame seeds.

In a separate small bowl, combine the white and black sesame seeds.

Shape 1½ Tbsp of dough into a ball, roll it in the sesame seed mixture, and place it onto the lined baking sheet. Using the flat bottom of a glass or measuring cup, gently press the cookie ball until it's about ⅓ inch thick. Repeat with the remaining cookie dough and refrigerate for about 15 minutes.

While the cookies are chilling, preheat the oven to 350°F.

Bake the cookies for 8–10 minutes, until slightly spread out and light golden brown on top.

Immediately out of the oven, the cookies will be very soft. Allow them to cool on the baking sheet for about 10 minutes before transferring them to a cooling rack to cool completely. They keep well in a cool dry place in a closed container for about 1 week.

BLUEBERRY SOUR CREAM PIE

MAKES ONE 9-INCH PIE

Admittedly, making pie is a bit of a commitment, but I promise you that the time and effort involved are worth it. Obviously a batch of freshly picked wild blueberries are the ideal dream ingredient to use here, but in all honesty, you're going to have a winner on your hands even if you only have access to the frozen kind. The streusel topping is a great recipe to use any time you want to mix things up in your pie repertoire and move to a crumbly, oat-y topper instead of pastry. Have the kids roll the pastry base out when it's ready to save yourself a bit of work. Their little hands are also good for mixing the butter into the rest of the streusel ingredients.

½ batch Flaky Pastry (page 220)

FILLING

1 cup full-fat sour cream

1 egg

⅔ cup sugar

2 Tbsp all-purpose flour

1 tsp grated lemon zest

1 tsp vanilla extract

¼ tsp kosher salt

3 cups fresh or frozen wild
    blueberries

STREUSEL

⅓ cup all-purpose flour

⅓ cup packed brown sugar

¼ cup rolled oats, not instant

¼ tsp cinnamon

⅓ cup cold cubed butter

Preheat the oven to 425°F. Make the flaky pastry. While that rests in the fridge, make the filling.

In a bowl, whisk together the sour cream, egg, sugar, flour, lemon zest, vanilla, and salt until smooth, then fold in the blueberries.

On a lightly floured work surface, roll the rested pastry into a 12-inch circle, about ¼ inch thick. Gently transfer the pastry into a 9-inch pie dish, making sure to press the dough into the edges of the pan and letting it come up the sides and rest over the lip of the pan. You can crimp the edges or leave it rustic. Transfer the pie dough to the fridge to firm up for at least 15 minutes.

Pour the filling into the pie shell. Bake the pie directly on the bottom of the oven, for 15 minutes. This helps to crisp up the bottom of the pie crust.

Meanwhile, for the streusel, in a medium bowl, whisk together the flour, brown sugar, oats, and cinnamon. Using your fingers, rub in the butter until the mixture resembles coarse crumbs. Sprinkle the streusel evenly over the par-baked pie shell.

Reduce the oven temperature to 350°F, covering the crust with aluminum foil if it appears to be browning too quickly. Bake for 40 minutes, until the filling is puffed and set but still jiggly in the center and the pastry is a deep golden brown. Remove the pie from the oven and allow to cool on the counter. Serve at room temperature. This is especially good with the Lemon & Sour Cream Ice Cream (page 125). Leftovers can be stored at room temperature for a few days, if it lasts that long.

WEEKNIGHTS

"IF YOU ARE A CHEF, NO MATTER HOW GOOD A CHEF YOU ARE, IT'S NOT GOOD COOKING FOR YOURSELF; THE JOY IS IN COOKING FOR OTHERS."

—NOTED CULINARY PHILOSOPHER WILL.I.AM

Conquering weeknight meals is one of the most gratifying and useful things a culinary dad can do, and having a solid repertoire of go-to dishes makes that a snap.

To qualify as a seamless, satisfying, and delicious weeknight dinner, there are a few criteria: it has to be fairly easy to execute. It has to be balanced and mostly healthy but also fun and a pleasure to eat. It needs to be family-friendly and have an accessible price point. It should involve little to no shopping, create a minimal amount of mess, and be made from accessible pantry ingredients. You don't want to be hitting up three different grocery stores in order to get that one obscure specialty item, if you can avoid it.

Even with all those stipulations, there's still plenty of runway to be creative.

The biggest secret to efficient weekday cooking, though, is to cook once in order to eat twice, and each of the following recipes is designed with the idea of leftovers in mind. Although our preference is to cook from scratch whenever possible, a freezer full of delicious meals is a great safety net to have around for those evenings when there's just too much going on.

FRIED QUESO WITH CHILI OIL, LIME, CILANTRO & GREEN ONIONS

SERVES 4

Any time Martina and I are making anything even remotely Mexican-inspired, we're going to be searing up a plate of this. To be honest, it probably shows up more often just on its own as a midday or late-night snack. With its browned exterior and molten, cheesy interior, it's like saganaki meets Cinco de Mayo. Of course, melted cheese has a 100% success rate with kids, and Barlow loves to squeeze the lime juice and sprinkle the cilantro overtop when it's done. Depending on your kids' spice preference, you could seed and devein the jalapeño, soak it in water for a bit to lessen the bite, or, in a pinch, remove it altogether.

10 oz queso fresco or halloumi

1 tsp vegetable oil

¼ cup picked cilantro leaves

1 green onion, thinly sliced

½ lime

½ jalapeño, thinly sliced

½ Tbsp Pasilla Chili Oil (page 227)

Cut the cheese into ½-inch slices. In a nonstick or cast-iron pan, heat the oil over medium-high heat until it shimmers, then add the cheese. Cook until deep brown on both sides, about 2 minutes per side, then arrange on a plate and garnish with the cilantro, green onions, a squeeze of lime juice, sliced jalapeños, and a few drops of pasilla oil. For fun, let the kids sprinkle on the garnishes and squeeze the lime juice themselves.

SWEET PEA HUMMUS

Poor hummus. Has any dish been more widely abused this century? Nobody asked for cake-batter or chocolate-mint or pizza-flavored hummus, but they all exist. While this version might not be as outrageous as those, it's not entirely traditional either. I use the sweet peas here in the same way I use them in the Sweet Pea & Avocado Guacamole (page 45)—to boost the vibrancy of the dish and make it a bit healthier, lighter, and fresher. The finished recipe lasts for a few days in the fridge and makes a beautiful dip for crisp vegetables, but I especially love it as the anchor for the Baked Halibut (page 183), where it soaks up all the juices from the fish and becomes an incredible, impressive sauce that takes about 5 minutes of prep. This recipe makes a lot of hummus, so feel free to adjust the amount based on your needs.

MAKES ABOUT 4 CUPS

½ cup olive oil

½ cup tahini

Juice of 3 lemons

1¼ cups canned chickpeas, rinsed and drained

1¼ cup frozen sweet peas

1 clove garlic

1 cup packed coarsely chopped parsley

¼ cup packed coarsely chopped mint

2 tsp kosher salt

In a food processor or blender, combine all the ingredients, putting the liquid ingredients in first. Process until the hummus is smooth and homogeneous. Keep in an airtight container in the fridge for up to 3 days.

CRUSHED CUCUMBER SALAD

SERVES 4

When I started out cooking at Scaramouche in the late '90s, this often appeared as part of our staff meal before the shift started. Depending on who was cooking, you'd get flavors and dishes from all over the world. We'd gather together every night before the craziness in the kitchen began to enjoy a civilized moment together. This was always one of my favorite sides, made by an old friend.

6 Persian cucumbers or
   1 English cucumber

1 Tbsp apple cider vinegar

2 Tbsp rice wine vinegar

1 Tbsp sesame oil

1 Tbsp soy sauce

1½ tsp sugar

1 tsp kosher salt

1 clove garlic, minced

½ cup coarsely chopped cilantro

2 Tbsp mixed black and white
   sesame seeds

1 Tbsp of your favorite chili oil, for
   garnish

Using a rolling pin or a heavy wooden spoon, lightly crush the cucumbers with enough force to split them somewhat. Give them a quarter turn and bash them again. You're not looking to pulverize the cucumbers, just bruise them a bit. Cut the cucumbers into 1-inch pieces on a bias.

For the dressing, in a large bowl, combine the vinegars, sesame oil, soy sauce, sugar, salt, and garlic. Toss the cucumbers in the dressing to coat, then garnish with cilantro and sesame seeds.

TOMATO SALAD WITH AVOCADO RANCH

SERVES 4

2 large heirloom tomatoes, room temperature

½ pint cherry tomatoes

Flaky salt

Buttermilk Avocado Ranch (page 225)

Black pepper

¼ cup packed basil leaves

1 Tbsp chopped chives

Extra-virgin olive oil

In prime tomato season, when the fruit is at its absolute peak, my philosophy is that the less you manipulate it, the better. This recipe illustrates that in a very delicious way. It really doesn't matter what kind of tomatoes you use here—cherry tomatoes, Romas, or big beefsteak-style bruisers. The main thing, as with any tomato salad, is to slice them out on a platter and salt them a good 20 minutes in advance to allow that seasoning to start pulling some of those juices out. All that lovely concentrated tomato flavor will start to pool on the bottom of the plate and act as kind of a backbone to the dressing. Speaking of dressing, everybody's done tomatoes with balsamic and olive oil, but here we're using one of my favorite dressings and one that shows up a few times in this book (Cali-Inspired Avocado Ranch Salad, page 38; Roasted Sweet Potatoes, page 46; and Fried Green Tomatoes, page 138). If you've got the dressing in the fridge, you've got a great dinner-party or quick dinner dish ready to go in a flash.

Cut the heirloom tomatoes into ½-inch slices and the cherry tomatoes into halves, and arrange in a single layer on a platter. Season generously with salt and allow to sit for 20 minutes. This allows the seasoning to penetrate and acts as a sort of curing process.

After the tomatoes have cured, dress generously with the avocado ranch. Season with pepper, basil, chives, and a drizzle of olive oil.

FRENCH BISTRO SALAD

SERVES 4

2 heads butter lettuce,
  leaves separated

3 radishes, thinly sliced

2 Tbsp picked tarragon leaves

2 Tbsp chopped chives,
  cut into 1-inch batons

⅓ cup Apple, Thyme & Shallot
  Vinaigrette (page 224) or
  Buttermilk Avocado Ranch
  (page 225)

Kosher salt

Although this is an exceedingly simple salad, it always brings me back to one of my favorite meals of all time at one of my favorite restaurants on earth: Le Coq Rico. If I could transport one restaurant that I've experienced overseas to my home city, that would definitely be the one. Le Coq Rico is an exceptional Parisian rotisserie chicken restaurant that was a major inspiration for Flock. The menu comprises a bunch of different kinds of chickens— Bresse, Noire de Challans, Forez. No matter which one you order, it comes with fries and a salad with a simple vinaigrette and some chives, very much like this one. Add a perfectly roasted chicken, like my Flock Spiced Grilled Spatchcocked Chicken (page 200), and it's the quintessential Sunday spread for me.

Place a few leaves of butter lettuce in a serving bowl or on a platter, layering with radish slices, tarragon, and chives. Continue building to make a nice, high pile.

Drizzle generous amounts of the dressing over and around the lettuce and finish with a pinch of kosher salt. Serve a little extra dressing on the side.

CRUNCHY CABBAGE & APPLE SLAW WITH HONEY GREEN HERB DRESSING

SERVES 4

¼ head red cabbage

¼ head savoy cabbage

1 tsp kosher salt

1 Tbsp red wine vinegar

1 cup picked and torn parsley leaves

½ green apple, julienned

2 green onions, thinly sliced

½ cup Green Tahini Dressing (page 225)

1 Tbsp black sesame seeds

½ cup roasted and coarsely chopped cashews

We buy red cabbage for different recipes, but there always seems to be a little more than we can get through. So turning it into a quick slaw to pair with a great sandwich or just have on its own makes sure none of it goes to waste. I always salt and vinegar the slaw well before I dress it, which helps it break down and bring the purple color all through the dish. At dinnertime, we often find ourselves counting the colors on our plate, and here, there are about 10 different shades. This slaw is great for kids because they like looking at all the elements within it and configuring each bite for themselves.

Thinly slice the red and savoy cabbage and toss in a large bowl with salt and red wine vinegar. Leave in the fridge for 30 minutes to 1 hour. Add the parsley, apples, green onions, and dressing and toss to coat. Garnish with sesame seeds and roasted cashews.

KITCHEN TIP: This is a dead-easy salad and, once again, the star of this one is the dressing. People think of dressings and vinaigrettes as "for salad," but they're so much more versatile than that. Green Tahini is not only a striking salad dressing but also a great base to toss roasted vegetables in, and I've even brushed it on a glaze for salmon on the broiler. It's got a bright green, zippy flavor and a good 3-day life span in the fridge before the color starts to fade.

BRAISED CHICKEN, ANCHO & TOMATILLO SOUP

SERVES 6 + LEFTOVERS

This is one of my all-time favorite recipes. It was on the Harbord Room menu for about 2 weeks, but somehow dropped off. It might be because it's one of those recipes that just works better when cooked at home rather than in a restaurant. I recently remembered it and couldn't believe I'd gone so long without making it again. I happened to have all the ingredients on hand and it came back to me in a flash. It felt like running into an old friend. Basically, it's a full-bodied one-pot-wonder soup that also eats like a meal. I keep it at about a three or four on the spice scale so that it stays kid-friendly. To make it a meal, serve it with rice or hominy. It also freezes well, so make a large batch, because you're going to want to have leftovers.

3 Tbsp olive oil + extra for garnish

8 bone-in, skinless chicken thighs

Kosher salt and black pepper

1½ lb tomatillo, husks removed and cut in half

1 large Spanish onion, sliced

3 cloves garlic, chopped

1 poblano pepper, seeded and sliced

½ Tbsp ancho chili powder (see tip)

½ cup dry white wine

1 ripe plantain, peeled and cut in 1-inch pieces

3 cups chicken stock

One 14 oz can full-fat coconut milk , divided

1 cup packed picked cilantro leaves + extra for garnish

Zest and juice of 1 lime

1 cup crumbled queso fresco or feta

½ cup toasted crushed peanuts

Red chilies, sliced, for garnish

KITCHEN TIP: If you are heat-sensitive when it comes to spice, you can remove either the poblano pepper or the ancho chili powder.

Heat a large heavy-bottomed pot over medium-high heat with 3 Tbsp olive oil. Season the chicken with salt and pepper. Cook the chicken on each side until golden brown, about 2 minutes per side. Take the time to brown the chicken properly, as this will add so much richness to the end product.

Transfer the chicken to a plate and add the tomatillo, onions, garlic, and poblano peppers to the pot along with a generous pinch of salt and the ancho chili powder. Reduce the heat to medium and cook until the tomatillos, peppers, and onions fully soften and begin to color, about 7 minutes.

Add the white wine and plantains. Boil the mixture until the liquid reduces by half, then add the chicken back to the pot along with the chicken stock and 12½ oz of coconut milk. The liquid should just cover the top of the chicken, and you can add a little water or extra stock if it's not quite covering.

Place a tight-fitting lid on the pot and cook on low heat for 45 minutes, or until the chicken begins to pull away from the bone. Carefully remove the chicken and let it cool slightly. Remove the chicken from the bone and tear or shred into bite-sized pieces.

Add the 1 cup of cilantro and the lime zest and juice to the pot and coarsely puree the soup using an immersion blender (or transfer to a stand-up blender and puree, in batches if necessary). Make sure to keep a fair bit of texture within it. Check the soup for seasoning and adjust the salt level according to your taste. Add the pulled chicken back to the pot and heat it up, then serve with a drizzle of the remaining coconut milk and olive oil, the crumbled cheese, peanuts, fresh cilantro, and sliced chilies.

ONE-POT BRAISED TURKEY MEATBALLS

SERVES 6

Even though I didn't eat this at all as a kid, this dish reminds me so much of my childhood and my mother's home cooking—it's the quintessential '80s dish. There's just something about the look and feel of this dish that's so comforting and familiar. It's a one-pot meal that carries over into leftovers really well. It also helps that it's one of those things that Barlow loves; for weekday cooking, one of the main questions I ask myself before making a recipe is, will my kid eat this? I'd say I've got a 90% success rate with this one.

MEATBALLS

1½ lb ground turkey

1 egg

½ cup seasoned breadcrumbs

⅓ cup grated Parmigiano-Reggiano

½ onion, minced

1 tsp kosher salt

½ tsp black pepper

¼ cup finely chopped parsley

½ tsp dried oregano

1½ tsp Worcestershire sauce

2 Tbsp olive oil

RICE

1 Tbsp olive oil

½ onion, minced

1 clove garlic, minced

1½ cups long-grain brown rice

½ tsp fennel seeds

Pinch chili flakes

1 bay leaf

4 cups chicken stock

Juice of 1 lemon

3 cups packed spinach

½ cup crumbled feta

1 Tbsp butter

In a large mixing bowl, combine the turkey, egg, breadcrumbs, parm, onions, salt, pepper, parsley, oregano, and Worcestershire sauce. Using a wooden spoon or sturdy spatula, beat the mixture vigorously until well mixed and uniform in consistency. Shape the turkey into golf-ball-sized balls; you should get around 18 pieces.

In a heavy-bottomed braising pot over medium heat, heat 2 Tbsp olive oil. Working in batches, brown the meatballs on all sides, then remove from the pot and set aside. At this point, the meatballs can be frozen for later use.

In the same pot, combine 1 Tbsp olive oil, the onion, and garlic and cook over medium heat until softened, about 5 minutes. Add the rice, fennel seeds, chili flakes, and bay leaf and stir to coat. Add the stock and lemon juice. Cover and cook for 15 minutes on low heat. Remove the lid, add the browned meatballs on top, and replace the lid. Cook on low for an additional 15 minutes, or until the rice is tender and the meatballs are completely cooked through.

When the meatballs are cooked through, turn off the heat and add the spinach, crumbled feta, and butter. Stir once, just to wilt the spinach, and serve.

LITTLE PASTA WITH SWISS CHARD & LENTILS

SERVES 4

LENTILS

1 bunch Swiss chard

4 sprigs thyme

2 sprigs rosemary

1 medium onion, minced

2 stalks celery, finely chopped

2 medium carrots, finely chopped

2 cloves garlic, minced

2 Tbsp olive oil

2 tsp kosher salt

1 tsp black pepper

½ tsp allspice

⅛ tsp ground cloves

1 bay leaf

3 strips lemon peel

½ cup dry red wine (optional)

4 cups chicken or vegetable stock

1½ cups Puy lentils

Parmigiano-Reggiano rind
    (optional)

FOR SERVING

8 oz small pasta (tubetti, ditalini,
    orzo)

Toasted Sourdough Breadcrumbs
    with Rosemary & Sea Salt
    (page 228)

Grated Parmigiano-Reggiano

Fermented Red Chilies (page 227)

This dish was inspired by Martina, who was inspired by cleaning out our fridge, which is, after all, how a lot of great home-cooked recipes are created. It's a quintessential winter dish, warming and hearty, and also dead simple: chard, pasta, lentils. Ultimately, it's a type of *cucina povera*, but that doesn't mean it can't be elevated. The flavor comes from the allspice and cloves, which aren't traditional in pasta dishes but are not at all uncommon with lentil dishes. Kids seem to love the small pasta because they can get a good bite on a spoon, and it's fun for them to stir everything together so the cheese emulsifies with the broth. It's definitely been one of our staples for the past couple of years, Barlow loves it, and it lasts in the fridge for a good few days, so we usually make twice as much as we need—I also use the lentils as the base for the Braised Lamb Shank Soup on page 152.

Remove the leaves from the stalks of Swiss chard. Finely dice the stems and set aside. Cut the leaves into thin ribbons and set aside in a separate bowl. Remove the leaves from the thyme and rosemary and finely chop. Set aside.

In a heavy-bottomed pot, combine the onions, celery, carrots, garlic, Swiss chard stems, thyme, rosemary, olive oil, salt, and pepper. Cook over medium heat until the veggies begin to sweat, about 5 minutes. Add the allspice, cloves, bay leaf, and lemon peel. When the vegetables are soft and translucent, add the red wine and cook until almost completely reduced, then add the stock. Add the lentils and Parmigiano-Reggiano rind. Cover and cook over medium heat for 30 minutes, until the lentils are just tender and still covered by the liquid.

Meanwhile, cook the pasta in boiling salted water until al dente, following the package instructions.

When the lentils are ready, add the chard leaves and remove from the heat.

To serve, add the cooked hot pasta to the pot with the lentils and stir to combine. There should still be some residual broth in the pot, so make sure to add some broth to each serving. Garnish with the toasted sourdough breadcrumbs and a generous grating of Parmigiano-Reggiano. Serve with fermented chilies.

CRISPY-SKIN SALMON WITH CHANTERELLE MUSHROOM & SOY VINAIGRETTE

SERVES 4

Four 4–5 oz center-cut salmon fillets, skin on

¼ cup olive oil, divided

2 Tbsp minced shallots

1 tsp grated ginger

1 tsp finely chopped garlic

3 sprigs thyme, leaves picked and chopped

½ lb (about 3 cups) chanterelle mushrooms, brushed clean of any dirt and thinly sliced

3 Tbsp cider vinegar or white wine vinegar

3 Tbsp soy sauce

1 Tbsp maple syrup

Juice of 1 lemon

Kosher salt and black pepper, to taste

2 Tbsp canola oil

FOR SERVING

2 bunches spinach, sautéed until wilted in a little olive oil with salt and pepper

Flaky salt

A beautiful piece of salmon with a crispy skin, dressed with a substantial vinaigrette, is a really satisfying way take your fish game to the next level. Here I'm using beautiful, tender, golden-yellow chanterelles for their unique, peachy-corn flavor and all-around awesomeness. Set the kids up with a brush and have them gently clean the mushrooms for you while you get the other ingredients ready and that hands-on experience will make even the most mycophobic child much more likely to give them a try. If chanterelles aren't readily available, go ahead and substitute button, or oyster, or whatever's handy.

Make sure your salmon has been scaled—if not, run the back of a knife across the scales until they are all removed. Rinse the fish under cold water and dry very thoroughly with paper towel. One of the key points to achieving that golden crispy skin is starting with a very dry surface.

Using a sharp knife, carefully make one slit down the skin lengthwise—be sure just to puncture the skin, barely going into the flesh. This will help the skin stay flat as the fish contracts in the hot pan.

Set the fish aside and preheat the oven to 425°F.

In a large sauté pan on medium-high heat, heat 2 Tbsp olive oil. When the oil is hot, add the shallots and cook until just softened, about 2 minutes. Add the ginger, garlic, and thyme and cook for another 2 minutes, until translucent but not browned. Add the sliced chanterelles and cook, stirring, until they are cooked through and tender. Deglaze the hot pan with your vinegar and soy sauce, stirring all of the cooked flavorful bits off the bottom. Add the remaining 2 Tbsp olive oil, maple syrup, and lemon juice, and season with salt and pepper. Reserve at room temperature until ready to serve.

For the salmon, in a large cast-iron pan over medium-high heat, heat the canola oil. Season your fish with salt and pepper. Wait for the oil to just begin to smoke, then carefully lay your salmon in the pan, skin side down. Do not move the salmon once it touches down in the pan. Using your spatula, firmly press down on the salmon to ensure the skin is in direct contact with the hot pan—it will have a tendency to curl and contract once it hits the heat. Keep cooking for 2 minutes or until the edges begin to brown.

Transfer the pan to the hot oven and cook for 4–8 minutes depending on your preferred doneness—I like mine on the medium side.

Remove the fish using a flat spatula, taking care not to tear the skin. Serve on a platter over sautéed spinach, spoon a generous amount of the chanterelle vinaigrette over and around the fish, and add a spattering of flaky salt to finish.

WARM POTATO SALAD

RED PEPPER, COCONUT, SWEET POTATO & CHICKPEA CURRY

SERVES 6 + LEFTOVERS

1 red pepper, ¼-inch diced

2 jalapeños, seeded and finely chopped, or to taste (see tip)

1 leek (white and pale green parts only), split lengthwise and finely sliced

2 cloves garlic, chopped

3 Tbsp olive oil

1½ Tbsp mild curry powder

1 bay leaf

1 Tbsp grated ginger

1 stalk celery, ¼-inch diced

1 sweet potato, peeled and ¼-inch diced

2 tsp kosher salt

1 tsp black pepper

2 cups canned chickpeas, rinsed and drained

3½ cups vegetable stock

One 14 oz can full-fat coconut milk

1 cup chopped canned plum tomatoes

½ cup picked cilantro leaves

1 lime, cut in wedges

What I love about this soup, beyond the great flavor, is how completely simple it is and how quickly it comes together. The sweet potato breaks down a bit as it cooks and adds a nice body to the stew. It works great as a hybrid lunch, on its own or with a salad, or you could add in some brown rice to make it a complete meal. Here, I'm giving you a pretty large batch size because it reheats and freezes well, so it's easy to pull off when you're in a hurry. If you want to make it a little fancier, you could add a drizzle of coconut milk overtop, or get one of the kids to do it—they tend to have a knack for that kind of thing.

In a medium heavy-bottomed pan over medium heat, sweat the red peppers, jalapeños, leeks, and garlic in the olive oil until just tender, about 5 minutes. Add the curry powder, bay leaf, and ginger and toast until fragrant, about 2 minutes. Add all the remaining ingredients except for the cilantro and lime, and stir to combine.

Reduce the heat to medium-low and simmer for 25–30 minutes, until the sweet potatoes are fully softened. If you're eating this as your main course, serve it over steamed rice. Garnish with a generous amount of freshly picked cilantro and a lime wedge to squeeze overtop.

KITCHEN TIP: If you are heat-sensitive, try this recipe without the jalapeños, or with just one.

FULLY LOADED SWEET POTATO TACOS

SERVES 4

4 sweet potatoes

½ cup olive oil

1 tsp kosher salt

2 tsp chili powder, divided

2 cups crumbled cotija cheese

Pasilla Chili Oil (page 227; optional)

1 cup shredded red cabbage

2 radishes, thinly sliced

½ cup thinly sliced green onions

½ cup full-fat sour cream

1 lime, quartered

This is another example of a fridge clean-out session resulting in a bold and colorful meal Martina and I return to again and again. You can use everything and anything in your own fridge. As we found, it turns out that baked sweet potatoes, with their super-soft, molten, creamy interior, are a stellar item to showcase taco toppings: cheese, red cabbage, radishes, green onions, and sour cream. If you want to go the extra mile and make salsa, all the better. Baked potatoes are usually such a winter dish, but by dressing them up this way, they take on a more summery vibe. They're ultra-satisfying and can be a meal on their own, but they're also great served as a side dish with a roasted rotisserie chicken. Much like tacos, this meal becomes a family-style "make your own" event and makes for a nice interactive dinner for the kids.

Preheat the oven to 400°F and line a baking sheet with aluminum foil.

Using a fork, puncture a series of holes evenly all over the sweet potatoes, and place them on the lined baking sheet. In a small bowl, combine the olive oil, salt, and 1 tsp chili powder. Drizzle the oil mixture over the potatoes, then rub it over to coat. Bake the potatoes for about 1 hour, or until they have completely softened.

Remove the potatoes from the oven and allow them to cool slightly before slicing them lengthwise on one side (just deep enough that they are able to open easily). Sprinkle the cotija evenly inside the potatoes (½ cup cheese per potato), drizzle with pasilla oil, and sprinkle with the remaining 1 tsp chili powder. Return to the oven until the cheese is bubbly, about 5 minutes.

Garnish with the red cabbage, radish slices, green onions, sour cream, and a wedge of lime.

BAKED SHELLS WITH ZUCCHINI, RICOTTA & PEAS

Conchiglie rigate, lumaconi gigante, tufoli, or the anglicized "jumbo shells" are all wonderful pasta shapes that revel in this creamy, bright, summery stuffing. While not exactly spa food, this is definitely on the lighter side as far as baked pasta goes, thanks to the grated zucchini and the almost pureed peas. Feel free to make your own tomato sauce and really lean into the recipe, or call in a jar of good-quality store-bought. Because the bulk of the preparation can be done well ahead of time, it's a great dish for entertaining that requires next to no monitoring once it's in the oven.

SERVES 6

1 medium zucchini, grated

2 tsp kosher salt, divided,
   + extra to taste

1 cup frozen or blanched
   sweet peas

Zest of 2 lemons

1 cup packed parsley leaves

1 cup packed basil leaves
   + extra for garnish

½ tsp black pepper + extra
   to taste

1½ cups full-fat dry ricotta
   (see tip on page 133)

1½ cups grated Parmigiano-
   Reggiano, divided, + extra
   for garnish

1 egg

½ tsp freshly grated nutmeg

2 cups tomato sauce, homemade
   or your favorite store-bought

1 lb large pasta shells, cooked
   al dente and cooled

1 ball fresh mozzarella, torn

2 Tbsp olive oil

In a bowl, combine the grated zucchini with 1 tsp salt, and let sit for 15 minutes. Using a cheesecloth or paper towel, wring out the excess water from the zucchini and set aside in a large bowl.

In a blender or food processor, combine the peas, lemon zest, parsley, basil, remaining 1 tsp salt, and pepper. Pulse until the mixture is not quite pureed. Add the pea mixture to the bowl with the zucchini, along with the ricotta, 1 cup Parmigiano-Reggiano, egg, and nutmeg. Mix until everything is evenly incorporated, then season with salt and pepper to taste.

In a large casserole dish, spread the tomato sauce out to completely cover the bottom. Spoon the ricotta filling into the cooked shells so they are full but not overflowing, and nestle the stuffed shells on top of the sauce (they should fit snugly). Top with torn mozzarella and the remaining ½ cup parm, and drizzle with olive oil. Cover with aluminum foil and keep in the fridge until ready to bake. This can be done the day before, or even stored in the freezer at this stage.

When ready to bake, preheat the oven to 375°F. Bake, covered, for 30 minutes, then uncover and bake for an additional 30 minutes, until brown and bubbly on top (if baking from frozen, bake for 10 minutes more). Garnish with fresh basil and more shaved parm if desired.

HERB & ROASTED CAULIFLOWER SALAD

SERVES 4–6

Roasting cauliflower in a hot oven completely transforms the humble brassica into something dark, rich, and profound. A bowl full of caramelized florets with just a little salt, pepper, and olive oil is delicious on its own, but toss them with a creamy, slightly spicy dressing, a sprinkling of dried fruit, and heaps of fresh herbs, and you've got a blockbuster on your hands. This recipe was inspired by Sami Tamimi and Tara Wigley's incredible cookbook, *Falastin*, where they use yogurt as a cauliflower marinade.

1 shallot, thinly sliced

1 red chili, thinly sliced

⅓ cup dried cherries, cranberries, or raisins

¼ cup white wine vinegar

1 Tbsp honey

¼ cup full-fat mayonnaise

¼ cup full-fat sour cream

3 Tbsp olive oil

1 Tbsp cumin seeds

1 tsp chili powder

1 tsp kosher salt

½ tsp turmeric

1 large head cauliflower, broken into bite-sized pieces

1 cup packed basil leaves, torn

1 cup packed mint leaves, torn

¼ cup toasted pine nuts

Preheat the oven to 475°F.

In a small bowl, combine the shallots, red chilies, dried fruit, vinegar, and honey. Allow to sit at room temperature for 1–5 hours.

In a large bowl, combine the mayonnaise, sour cream, olive oil, cumin seeds, chili powder, salt, and turmeric. Add the cauliflower to the mayonnaise mixture and massage until each piece is well coated. Roast in a single layer on a baking sheet for about 12 minutes, until very dark golden brown and still crunchy. Remove from the oven and let cool completely.

When ready to serve, toss the cauliflower with basil and mint leaves. Arrange on a platter and top with the pickled shallot mixture and toasted pine nuts.

ROASTED GLAZED BROCCOLI & CAULIFLOWER

SERVES 4–6

½ cup mayonnaise

⅓ cup nutritional yeast flakes (see sidebar)

1 Tbsp sriracha

1 tsp kosher salt

½ head broccoli

½ head cauliflower

1 cup canned chickpeas, rinsed and drained (optional)

These roasted vegetables have a serious craveable hook to them. The backbone is the mixture of mayonnaise, nutritional yeast, and sriracha, and the whole thing gets roasted in a hot oven so you get incredible caramelization, brown crispy bits, richness from the mayonnaise, heat from the sriracha, and tons of umami flavor from the yeast. It could not be easier to make, and it's a great kid-friendly side dish. It can also be used as part of a rice bowl or any of the salads—particularly the Cali-Inspired Avocado Ranch Salad (page 38). Swap out regular mayo for vegan mayo if you want to make this 100% vegan.

Preheat the oven to 400°F and line a baking sheet with parchment paper.

In a large bowl, combine the mayo, nutritional yeast, sriracha, and salt.

Break the broccoli and cauliflower into large florets. Add the broccoli, cauliflower and chickpeas to the bowl with the mayonnaise mixture and toss until each piece is fully coated. Spread evenly in a single layer on a baking sheet and roast for about 30 minutes, or until golden brown.

NUTRITIONAL YEAST: I use nutritional yeast quite often in soups, especially vegetarian and vegan soups, because it adds a lot of umami and depth of flavor. It's readily available at most grocery stores, and any health food or bulk store—and it's cheap. Use it like salt any time you're cooking a dish where a hard cheese might be a good partner—think roasted butternut squash soup, for example. It brings an almost Parmigiano-Reggiano flavor and richness while amplifying the flavors of the ingredients it's supporting.

STICKY SOY EGGPLANT

SERVES 4

1 Tbsp sugar

2 tsp cornstarch

⅓ cup soy sauce

⅓ cup water

¼ cup rice wine vinegar

4 Japanese eggplants or
   1 large Sicilian eggplant

1 bunch green onions

Neutral oil, for frying

2-inch knob peeled ginger,
   julienned

1 clove garlic, finely chopped

Sesame seeds, for garnish

This is my approach to a saucy, stir-fried eggplant dish, full of classic flavors like soy sauce, rice wine, ginger, garlic, and green onions. I'm calling for a nonstick pan here, but if you want to use cast-iron or a wok, feel free. If you haven't cooked a lot of eggplant before, this is an excellent place to start.

In a medium bowl, whisk together the sugar and cornstarch. Add the soy sauce, water, and rice wine vinegar. Mix until smooth and set aside.

Cut the eggplants into 1-inch cubes. Separate the white parts of the green onions from the green tops. Slice both portions finely and set aside separately.

To a large nonstick pan over medium-high heat, add enough cooking oil to generously coat the bottom of the pan. When the oil begins to shimmer, fry the eggplants in batches until golden brown on all sides and softened, 5–7 minutes, turning occasionally. Set aside. Lower the heat to medium and, in the remaining fat, gently fry the ginger, garlic, and white portions of the green onions for 1 minute, until fragrant. Add the fried eggplants back in and cook until tender, about 3 minutes. Pour the soy sauce mixture in and toss everything to incorporate. Cook for 1 minute, until thick and glossy.

Garnish with the tops of the green onions and the sesame seeds, and serve with rice.

APPLE FRANGIPANE GALETTE

SERVES 6

½ batch Flaky Pastry (page 220)

1½ cups Basic Frangipane (see below)

2 Granny Smith apples, peeled and thinly sliced (see tip)

2 Tbsp maple syrup

2 Tbsp cream or beaten egg, for egg wash

Pearl sugar, for sprinkling

The secret to making this into a quick weeknight recipe is to have a batch of premade frangipane already in the freezer. The basic recipe makes a double batch for this very reason. If you've also got the pastry in the freezer already, so much the better, but a store-bought frozen pastry would also work here in a pinch.

Preheat the oven to 350°F and line a baking sheet with parchment paper.

Roll out the pastry on a lightly floured surface to a 10-inch round, and place on the baking sheet. Spread the frangipane in the center of the pastry, leaving a 2- to 3-inch edge. Arrange the apples overtop the frangipane, then brush with maple syrup. Fold in the edges of the pastry to make a galette. Brush the exposed pastry with cream or egg, then sprinkle with pearl sugar.

Bake for 45–50 minutes, until the pastry is golden brown and the apples have softened.

BASIC FRANGIPANE

MAKES ABOUT 3 CUPS

2 cups almond flour

1 cup sugar, divided

¼ tsp kosher salt

1 cup butter, room temperature

3 tsp Grand Marnier

1 tsp vanilla extract

2 eggs, room temperature, divided

2 Tbsp milk

In a medium bowl, whisk together the almond flour with ¼ cup sugar and the salt. In a separate large bowl, beat the butter with the remaining ¾ cup sugar until light and creamy, about 5 minutes. Add the almond flour–sugar mixture and beat just until thoroughly combined. Add the Grand Marnier, vanilla, and 1 egg and mix just until incorporated. Add the milk and the second egg and mix until light and fluffy. Set aside to chill for at least 1 hour or overnight. The frangipane can be stored in the fridge for up to 3 days or frozen for up to 3 months.

KITCHEN TIP: This galette and frangipane base work with any stone fruit that's in season, so feel free to mix it up however you like.

RHUBARB CUSTARD PIE

SERVES 8

You can never have too many rhubarb recipes or too many pie recipes, and this version, built around a rich custard, is one of my favorite ways to eat spring's tastiest stalk. The sweet creaminess of the custard really balances out and supports the rhubarb's inherent tannic intensity.

½ batch Flaky Pastry (page 220)

1½ cups sugar

¼ cup all-purpose flour

¾ tsp freshly grated nutmeg

1 lb rhubarb, cut into 1-inch pieces (about 4 cups)

3 eggs, slightly beaten

3 Tbsp melted butter, cooled

Pearl sugar, for sprinkling

Preheat the oven to 400°F, with a rack on the bottom.

Roll out the pastry on a lightly floured surface into a circle about 12 inches in diameter, so that it will fit up the sides of a standard 9-inch pie plate and hang over the rim. Place the dough in the pie plate, crimp the edges, and chill for at least 30 minutes, or until ready to use.

In a large bowl, whisk together the sugar, flour, and nutmeg. Add the rhubarb and toss to coat. Add the eggs and melted butter and mix until fully incorporated. Pour into the chilled pie pastry and sprinkle with pearl sugar.

Bake on the lowest rack for 50–60 minutes, or until the pastry is golden brown. The pie can be stored at room temperature overnight.

ALMOND, BUCKWHEAT & CARDAMOM COOKIES

MAKES ABOUT 3 DOZEN COOKIES

½ cup coconut oil

3 Tbsp maple syrup

1 tsp vanilla extract

1 cup almond flour

1 cup buckwheat flour

1 cup unsweetened desiccated coconut

1 tsp cardamom

¼ tsp baking soda

¼ tsp kosher salt

If there's such a thing as a healthy cookie, this is it. Don't worry, it still tastes great. I love its inherently earthy, hoppy flavor; the fact that it's gluten-free and high in nutrients like potassium and essential amino acids is just an added bonus. On its own, the flour might be too much for a cookie like this, but the almond flour and coconut bring everything into balance. This is a very kid-friendly recipe, and little ones can participate in just about every aspect of the prep. It also makes for a great icebox cookie, where you can freeze a portion of the dough, then slice off and bake a few cookies whenever the mood strikes. These also go well as a kind of cracker for cheese.

Preheat the oven to 350°F.

In a small saucepan over low heat, combine the coconut oil, maple syrup, and vanilla and heat until melted and emulsified.

In a medium bowl, mix the remaining ingredients together with a wooden spoon. Pour the coconut oil mixture overtop and mix with a spoon until homogeneous (it will be a bit sandy).

Let the dough stand for 10 minutes to hydrate, then roll out half the dough between two pieces of parchment paper to ⅛ inch thick. (Roll the remaining dough into a 1½-inch thick log, wrap in plastic wrap, and freeze to easily slice and bake in the future. The dough can be stored in the freezer for up to 1 month.) Carefully transfer the bottom piece of parchment paper (with the rolled dough on top) to a baking sheet, and cut the dough into 1½-inch squares. You can bake them as is on the parchment sheet and then snap them apart once baked.

Bake for 15 minutes, or until light golden brown. The cookies can be stored in an airtight container at room temperature for up to 3 days.

WEEKEND PROJECTS

"MMM . . . DONUTS."

—HOMER SIMPSON

Dads bring the heat 110%, 24/7, 365. That's facts. But on the weekends, when they have time to stretch out a little bit, ease into the day, focus up, and take their time, that's when things really get interesting.

These recipes are for exactly those times. We're talking about a style of cooking that rewards patience and practice. These are not exactly 15-minute meals, but even the dishes that might take a little longer incorporate a lot of mostly unattended time, and none of these recipes requires any arcane culinary knowledge or super-specialized equipment. Some are even really easy; they just might look like they involved hours of prep and years of study to perfect.

Recipes like the ones in this chapter might involve making a special trip to the farmer's market for the highest-quality produce, or to the Mediterranean grocer for a fresh jar of tahini, or that new cheesemonger for something special. Those little adventures often lead to some amazing culinary discoveries anyway: a new type of heirloom tomato, a little shop you hadn't noticed before selling the best baklava—the kind scented with orange flower honey—or a favorite new Crottin de Chavignol.

Weekend cooking projects are primarily meant to be enjoyable and relaxed, offer big, flavorful results, and make the whole house smell incredible while you're at it. Get everyone together and have fun.

FRITTATA WITH FETA & ROMESCO SAUCE

SERVES 6

Knowing how to make a frittata is like having a culinary super-power. Once you've got the basic technique figured out—and there's really nothing to it—you can take it in a million different directions. It's a great way to clean out the fridge at the end of a long weekend at the cottage, for example. Throw in those left-over potatoes, or some of that barbecued salmon that somehow didn't get finished, along with whatever vegetables are still kicking around. This recipe shows what happens when you take a more formal approach, while giving you the basic fundamentals to improvise any which way you like in the future.

FRITTATA

7 eggs

¼ cup heavy cream

1 tsp kosher salt

2 Tbsp butter

2 medium yellow potatoes, sliced into ¼-inch rounds

2 zucchini, thinly sliced

4 sprigs thyme, leaves picked and chopped

2 cups baby spinach leaves

Black pepper

1 cup shredded cheddar

GARNISH

½ cup crumbled feta

½ cup Romesco Sauce (page 226)

3 radishes, thinly sliced

Drizzle of olive oil

¼ cup dill leaves

¼ cup parsley leaves

Preheat the oven to 375°F.

In a large bowl, whisk the eggs with the cream and salt, then set aside.

Heat the butter in a 10-inch cast-iron pan over medium heat. Add the potato slices in a single layer and cook for 3 minutes on each side, until browned and softened. Add the zucchini slices and thyme. Cook for 1 minute until softened, then stir in the spinach leaves to wilt. Crack some fresh pepper on top and evenly distribute the vegetables over the surface of the pan.

Pour the egg mixture overtop, then sprinkle with the cheddar. Cook on the stovetop for 3–4 minutes, until the edges just start to cook and brown. Transfer the pan to the oven and bake for 10–12 minutes, or until the center is just set, with no runny egg.

Let the frittata cool slightly for 5 minutes, then run a paring knife along the edge to release it and swiftly turn it out onto a cutting board or serving platter.

Garnish with a sprinkling of feta, a few dollops of romesco sauce, some sliced radishes, a drizzle of olive oil, and the herbs.

BASIC DONUTS

MAKES 1 DOZEN DONUTS

I don't think people consider making donuts at home as a viable project, but I'm here to tell you that not only can it be done, they're also going to be the best donuts of your life. If you can bake a loaf of bread or make a pie, you can make donuts. Hell, even if you can't do either of those things, you can make donuts. You've probably already got a stand mixer with a dough hook attachment from the wedding registry, and that's going to make life a lot easier for you with this recipe. Other than that, the only specialized equipment you might want are large and small metal rings. You'll also want a kitchen thermometer, but having one is pretty much standard, or should be, in the modern dad's kitchen anyway.

1½ Tbsp warm water

1 Tbsp + ½ tsp active dry yeast

½ cup milk

2 eggs

2 egg yolks

2¾ cups all-purpose flour

⅓ cup sugar

1 tsp kosher salt

½ cup butter, softened

Cooking spray

Vegetable oil, for frying

Milk Glaze (page 107)

Icing sugar, for dusting

Place the warm water in a small bowl and sprinkle the yeast overtop to activate it. In a stand mixer fitted with the dough hook attachment, mix the activated yeast. Add the milk, eggs, and egg yolks and mix to combine. Add the flour, sugar, and salt and mix on high speed until the dough comes together in a soft ball. Divide the butter into three equal portions and add to the dough in batches, mixing continuously. Make sure the butter is fully incorporated before adding the next portion.

When the butter is fully incorporated, continue to knead the dough for about 5 minutes, until sticky but soft. Place the dough in a lightly greased bowl, cover with plastic wrap, and rest in the fridge for 6 hours or overnight. Once chilled, you can freeze half of the dough in plastic wrap for another day.

While the dough rests, cut out 12 large squares of parchment paper, about 5 inches. Line a baking sheet with the parchment squares.

On a lightly floured surface, roll the dough into a large rectangle, ¾ inch thick, and use a large and small metal ring to punch out ring-shaped donuts (or cut into your desired shape using a knife). Place the donuts along with their cut-out centers on the parchment squares on the baking sheet, spray the tops with cooking spray, and cover lightly with plastic wrap. Allow them to proof in a warm place for 1 hour, or until doubled in size.

When the donuts have risen, line a plate with paper towel. In a large cast-iron pan over medium heat, heat 2 inches of oil to 350°F. You can test this by pinching off a small bit of dough and placing it in the oil; it should turn golden brown within 1 minute. Place a few donuts in the oil and fry for 1½ minutes per side, until golden brown with a lighter ring around the center. Once cooked, transfer the donuts to the paper towel–lined plate to cool slightly. Continue with the remaining donuts, adding more oil as needed and making sure to let the oil come back up to temperature between each batch.

Once cool enough to touch, dip the donuts in the glaze.

MILK GLAZE

MAKES ENOUGH FOR 1 DOZEN DONUTS

1 egg white, whipped to soft peaks

1 cup icing sugar

Juice of ½ lemon

¼ cup condensed milk

2 tsp freeze-dried raspberry powder (optional, see tip on page 130)

1½ Tbsp cocoa powder (optional)

Mix the egg white, icing sugar, lemon juice, and condensed milk in a large bowl. For a raspberry variation, add the raspberry powder, or for a chocolate variation, add the cocoa powder. If you like, you can make the glaze up to 1 day in advance and keep in the fridge.

BLUEBERRY SPELT MUFFINS

MARTINA'S BRAN MUFFINS WITH PRUNE BUTTER

MAKES 8–12 MUFFINS

When Martina and I first started dating, we decided to have a bran muffin bake-off—what can I say, I'm a romantic—because both of us claimed to produce the best version. Admittedly, despite not having had a bran muffin in the better part of a decade, I was feeling a bit cocky and went in cold, no recipe, just winging it. Martina, on the other hand, had spent a similar number of years carefully honing her recipe, tweaking it, and perfecting every nuance, and she absolutely came out swinging. Needless to say, her bran muffin was on another level altogether and was clearly the winner. Here it is.

⅓ cup pitted prunes

½ cup unsalted butter, softened

1 egg, lightly beaten

1 cup full-fat sour cream

¼ cup dark molasses

1 cup bran

½ cup raisins

1 tsp baking soda

¼ tsp kosher salt

1 cup all-purpose flour

Preheat the oven to 350°F and line a muffin tin with parchment paper slips.

In a small saucepan, place the prunes and add just enough water to cover. Simmer over medium heat until the prunes have softened and the water has almost fully evaporated. Drain and allow your prunes to cool to room temperature, about 15 minutes. In a blender or food processor, puree the prunes with the softened butter until smooth and fully incorporated. Split this mixture exactly in half, reserving half in a small jar as a spread.

Combine the remaining half of the prune-butter mixture with the egg, sour cream, molasses, bran, raisins, baking soda, and salt and mix by hand or with a beater until light and fluffy. Fold in the flour, taking care not to overmix.

Spoon the batter into the prepared muffin tin and bake for 15–18 minutes, or until just cooked in the center. Serve with the reserved spread.

KITCHEN TIP: I like to double up on the prune and butter mixture and save it to use on toast. If you want to add this easy step, use 1 cup softened, room-temperature butter and ⅔ cup pitted prunes.

BLUEBERRY SPELT MUFFINS

MAKES 6 XL MUFFINS

1 egg

⅔ cup plain, full-fat yogurt

5 Tbsp melted butter

⅓ cup maple syrup

Zest of 1 lemon

¼ tsp kosher salt

½ cup all-purpose flour

1 cup spelt flour

1½ tsp baking powder

¼ tsp baking soda

1½ cups frozen wild blueberries

½ cup good-quality granola,
    for garnish (optional)

This is a great recipe to get the kids involved in. Set them up on a stool and let them be the stir stars. Keep these muffins on hand for a quick on-the-go breakfast. If Martina and I take a road trip to see family out of town, these muffins are what I reach for to nosh on the way. By replacing all-purpose flour with spelt flour, we're also not trading health benefits for convenience. I'm partial to the frozen wild blueberries in this recipe because they're relatively inexpensive and pretty widely available, and they keep their integrity better than the big conventional ones that burst and bleed out into the muffin. We keep the blueberry-to-muffin ratio really high here, as it should be. This is not some gas-station muffin that's all cake.

Preheat the oven to 375°F. Butter or line your muffin tin with tall parchment paper slips.

In a large bowl, combine the egg, yogurt, melted butter, maple syrup, lemon zest, and salt and whisk until smooth. Sift in the all-purpose flour, spelt flour, baking powder, and baking soda. Gently fold the mixture over until it is just combined, taking care not to overmix. Add the frozen blueberries and stir once to distribute.

Divide the batter evenly between your prepared cups and sprinkle the tops with granola for a little extra crunch, about 1 Tbsp per muffin. Any extra muffin wells should be filled with a bit of water to avoid burning your pan. Your jumbo muffins might bake up together, with the sides touching, but that's all part of the fun. Any way you make them will be delicious.

Bake for about 20 minutes until browned and just cooked through in the center.

SHAVED BRUSSELS SPROUTS & LEEK PIZZA

MAKES TWO 10-INCH PIZZAS

This recipe is less about the ingredients and more about the technique. That said, I love making this in the fall, with the Gorgonzola and Brussels sprouts giving a real cold-weather feeling to the dish, but you can substitute ingredients that you or your family like. The Brussels sprout leaves and leeks get dressed with a bit of olive oil and salt and pepper, while a mix of garlic and shallots serve as the pie's base. Make sure to get your kid in the kitchen to help you pick the Brussels sprout leaves and eat dates (fiber!). The result is something that has as much in common with focaccia as it does with a classic pizza. If you've got a jar of the Fermented Red Chilies (page 227) in the fridge, this is an ideal base to slather some on.

One 1 lb ball pizza dough (page 112 or store-bought)

1 small shallot, thinly sliced

1 clove garlic, minced

½ tsp kosher salt

All-purpose flour, for shaping the dough

1 Tbsp vegetable oil

2 Tbsp olive oil

1 cup picked Brussels sprout leaves (about 10–12 sprouts), divided

1 large leek, white part only, washed and thinly sliced into rounds, divided

4 sprigs thyme, leaves picked, divided

¼ cup crumbled Gorgonzola, divided

Flaky salt, and black pepper

4 dates, pitted and sliced

Good-quality balsamic glaze

If making your own dough, follow the directions on page 112 until after the first rise. Wrap half of the homemade dough in plastic wrap and freeze for another use. Now, whether you're using the remaining homemade dough, or store-bought, halve the dough ball, place each half in separate lightly oiled mixing bowls, and cover loosely with plastic wrap. Leave the dough to rise at room temperature for about 2 hours.

In a bowl, stir to combine the shallots, garlic, and salt. Leave at room temperature for at least 10 minutes.

Once the dough has risen, heat a shallow 10-inch cast-iron pan over medium-low heat. While the pan is heating, turn your broiler on high and set your oven rack in the center of the oven.

On a floured surface, roll or stretch one dough ball out to the size of the pan. You are going for quite a thin crust here, so work gently and with patience to stretch the dough from the inside out. There are some great YouTube videos on how to do this.

Lightly brush the surface of the cast-iron pan with vegetable oil. Lay one portion of stretched dough on the hot surface, carefully using the handle of a wooden spoon to work it into the edges.

→ Continued . . .

Working quickly while your pan is still over medium-low heat, smear half of the minced shallot and garlic mixture around the base of the dough, followed by a drizzle of olive oil, and half of each of the Brussels sprout leaves, leeks, thyme, and crumbled Gorgonzola. Crank the heat to medium-high and cook the pizza for 1–2 minutes, until the bottom is lightly browned and crisp.

Transfer the pan to the oven and cook under the broiler for 3–4 minutes—you want the top to be slightly charred and bubbly. If it's getting too dark for your liking before it's crispy and cooked through, turn the broiler off and let the residual heat in the oven finish cooking the pizza for a few minutes.

Remove the pizza and finish with olive oil, flaky salt, fresh pepper, sliced dates, and some balsamic glaze. Serve hot to your family while you get back to work and make the second pizza.

PIZZA DOUGH

MAKES TWO 1 LB BALLS OF DOUGH

1 Tbsp honey

2¼ tsp (1 packet) active dry yeast

1⅔ cups warm water

4 cups all-purpose flour + extra as needed

1 Tbsp kosher salt

¼ cup olive oil

1½ Tbsp white wine vinegar

In a bowl, stir the honey and yeast together in the warm water; let the yeast bloom until it's bubbly, about 10 minutes.

Transfer your yeast mixture to a stand mixer fitted with the dough hook attachment. Add the flour, salt, olive oil, and vinegar and mix on medium speed for about 8 minutes, until smooth but slightly tacky. Alternatively, you can knead by hand: put the yeast mixture in a large bowl and stir in the flour, salt, olive oil, and vinegar. Transfer the dough to a clean work surface and knead for about 10 minutes, working the flour in as necessary, until you get a smooth and slightly tacky ball. Whichever method you use, the key is to work in as little extra flour as possible. If the dough is very sticky, you can mix in some extra flour a few teaspoons at a time, not exceeding ¼ cup extra in total.

Place the dough ball in a clean, lightly oiled bowl and cover with plastic wrap. Place the bowl in a warm area and let it rise for 1 hour, or until doubled in size. Punch it down. If you're not using the dough immediately, you can split the dough into two balls of about 1 lb each, wrap tightly in plastic, and freeze for up to 1 month.

If you're going to use the dough now, let it rise a second time for another hour, or until doubled in size, and then proceed with the recipe.

ROASTED EGGPLANT & HALLOUMI SALAD WITH GREEN TAHINI & HONEY DRESSING

SERVES 4

4 baby eggplants (see tip)

3 banana peppers

2 Tbsp olive oil

Kosher salt and black pepper

8 oz block halloumi, cut into
½-inch slices

½ batch Green Tahini Dressing
(page 225)

1 Tbsp honey

2 Tbsp white and/or black
sesame seeds

¼ cup picked and torn mint

¼ cup picked and torn cilantro

1 green onion, chopped

1 long red chili, chopped
(optional)

This was the dish that got my son, Barlow, to love eggplant. He already liked grilled halloumi drizzled with a bit of honey (who wouldn't?), so using that ingredient and combining it with the eggplant was a hook that gave him a way into the whole dish. Now he's an eggplant pro and loves the creamy, molten interior it gets, regardless of the preparation. When it comes to getting kids to try something new, you can sometimes overcome initial reluctance by serving it alongside a food they already love, rather than hiding the new ingredient. This recipe makes for a great light lunch on its own or is an excellent side dish for anything Mediterranean, like the Braised Lamb Shank Soup (page 152).

Preheat the oven to 400°F.

Keeping the eggplants whole, peel them from the cap down, until none of the skin remains. In a bowl, toss the peeled eggplants and banana peppers in olive oil and a few pinches of salt and pepper, then place them in a cast-iron pan. Roast until golden brown and completely tender, around 40 minutes, turning twice. Transfer the eggplants and peppers to a serving platter. In the same cast-iron pan, sear the halloumi on the stovetop over medium-high heat until golden on both sides, about 2 minutes per side.

Generously dress the eggplant and peppers with the tahini dressing, arrange the halloumi on top, and add more dressing. Drizzle the honey overtop and garnish with sesame seeds, mint, cilantro, green onions, and red chili.

KITCHEN TIP: The quality of your eggplants is what will take this dish from merely great to superstellar. Look for good, firm, heavy baby eggplants or the best in-season Japanese eggplants.

CAST-IRON BAKED EGGPLANT PARMESAN

SERVES 6

Olive oil

6 Japanese eggplants

Kosher salt

2 cups all-purpose flour

4 eggs, beaten

2 cups seasoned breadcrumbs

1 tsp fennel seeds

Handful torn basil leaves

4 cups tomato sauce (homemade or store-bought), divided, + extra for serving

12 oz low-moisture mozzarella (about 3 cups grated), divided

½ cup grated Parmigiano-Reggiano, divided, + extra for serving

Martina and I came up with this during the bad old days of full-on lockdown. We had some time on our hands, so we started playing around with eggplant parm and stumbled across this really fun way of preparing it. The key is to stack the eggplant into the pan very tightly. That way, when you turn it out, you get a spiraled dish where each slice comes off like petals. Another great thing about building the dish like this is that every ounce of sauce gets absorbed and the result is quite a firm parm that comes across almost like a savory cake.

Preheat the oven to 375°F and coat the bottom of a large baking sheet with olive oil.

Slice the eggplants lengthwise into ¼-inch slices. Generously salt both sides and place on paper towel to sit at room temperature for 15 minutes. This process helps to extract the excess liquid, impurities, and bitterness from the eggplants. Once the eggplants have released their liquid, rinse the slices under cold water and pat dry with a paper towel.

In three large dishes, arrange the flour, eggs, and breadcrumbs—this is your breading station. Coat each slice of eggplant first with flour, then egg, then breadcrumbs. Once each slice is breaded, lay on the oiled baking sheet.

When all the pieces of eggplant are breaded, drizzle them with more olive oil and bake until golden brown and crispy, about 20 minutes. Remove from the oven.

Meanwhile, in a 10-inch cast-iron pan over medium heat, lightly toast the fennel seeds. Add half of the torn basil. Cover the fennel and basil with 2 cups sauce, followed by one-third each of the mozzarella and Parmigiano-Reggiano. Arrange the eggplant in a coil above the sauce and cheese, keeping it as tightly packed as possible. Cover with the remaining 2 cups tomato sauce, followed by the remaining mozzarella, basil, and parm. Bake in the oven for 45 minutes, or until the cheese is golden brown and bubbly.

Remove the eggplant parm from the oven and allow to rest for 15 minutes before inverting onto a serving plate or cutting board. Slice and serve with more tomato sauce and grated Parmigiano-Reggiano.

PUMPKIN, CHESTNUT & CHORIZO SOUP

SERVES 6 + LEFTOVERS

This soup is an old Harbord Room staple that shines in the fall and into early winter when you get that first chill of the year. The heady spices, earthy textures, chestnuts, and spice in the chorizo all meld together. This is a chunky, coarse soup, not a puree, and it's the most warming bowl of soup I've ever had. It also proved to be a case study in what it means to balance a soup with a perfect level of heat, texture, and body. If you're ambitious, you can use fresh chestnuts that you roast and peel yourself, but any half-decent grocery store will sell packages of roasted and peeled chestnuts.

1 dried ancho chili

3 cups boiling water

¼ cup olive oil

1½ cups chopped white onions

1 medium carrot, diced

3 stalks celery, diced

3 oz (about ½ cup) sliced dry Spanish chorizo

2 tsp chopped thyme

¼ tsp ground cumin

¼ tsp ground coriander

¼ tsp ground fennel seeds

1 cup unsweetened pumpkin puree

1½ cups peeled chestnuts, coarsely chopped (preferably fresh; frozen or canned if necessary)

2 pinches saffron threads

1 cup canned whole peeled San Marzano tomatoes

4 cups low-sodium chicken stock

3 Tbsp sherry vinegar

Kosher salt and black pepper

GARNISH

½ cup crumbled fresh sheep's milk cheese

½ cup toasted pumpkin seeds

Good-quality olive oil

In a heatproof bowl, soak the ancho chili in the boiling water for 10 minutes. Drain and discard the soaking liquid. Remove and discard the seeds and stem.

In a large soup pot over medium heat, heat the olive oil. Add the onions, carrots, celery, and chorizo and cook for 4 minutes, or until the vegetables begin to sweat and soften. Add the thyme, cumin, coriander, and fennel seeds and cook 1 more minute, or until fragrant.

Add the pumpkin puree, chestnuts, saffron, tomatoes, stock, vinegar, and rehydrated ancho chili. Bring to a simmer and cook until the vegetables are tender and the flavors have combined, 20–30 minutes. Season with salt and pepper to taste.

Using an immersion blender, pulse the soup into a coarse, semi-chunky texture. Spoon into bowls and garnish with crumbled cheese, toasted pumpkin seeds, and a drizzle of olive oil.

SLOW-COOKED POLENTA

SUNDAY GRAVY

SERVES 6 + LEFTOVERS

Few things in this world make a house smell better than a big batch of Sunday gravy simmering away on the stove. Considering how utterly delicious and satisfying it is, there's really nothing to it. Gathering up all the ingredients is probably the biggest challenge to pulling this recipe off, and even that's pretty straightforward. This recipe makes a big batch. Sunday gravy seems to benefit from being made this way, and you benefit from being able to store leftovers in the freezer in 4-cup containers, so all the soulful comfort of Sunday gravy is available without any heavy lifting whatsoever.

2 Tbsp olive oil

1 small onion, finely chopped

3 cloves garlic, thinly sliced

½ tsp fennel seeds

Two 28 oz cans whole peeled San Marzano tomatoes

6 slices white bread, diced (3 cups)

1 cup milk

¾ lb ground beef

¾ lb ground pork

¾ lb ground veal

1 cup grated Parmigiano-Reggiano + extra for serving

⅓ cup chopped parsley

1 egg

½ tsp chili flakes

Zest of 1 lemon

1 tsp dried oregano

2 tsp kosher salt

1½ tsp ground black pepper

½ rack pork back ribs, cut between the bone into 2-inch sections

2 Italian sausages

½ cup picked basil leaves + extra for serving

1 bay leaf

In a Dutch oven or heavy-bottomed pot set over medium-low heat, add the olive oil, then add the onions, garlic, and fennel seeds. Cook until the onions and garlic have softened and the fennel seeds are fragrant. Add the tomatoes and cook for 20 minutes. Once the sauce has simmered, use an immersion blender to coarsely blend it to your desired consistency.

In a small bowl, combine the diced bread with milk and leave to soak for 30 minutes. After it has soaked, massage the bread and milk mixture until it has completely broken down into an oatmeal-like texture.

In a large bowl, combine the beef, pork, veal, Parmigiano-Reggiano, parsley, egg, chili flakes, lemon zest, oregano, salt, and pepper. Add the milk and bread mixture to this and massage vigorously until the mixture has emulsified and formed a tacky consistency. Using your hands, form the mixture into uniform balls, about 1½ inches in diameter.

When all the meatballs have been rolled, you can decide to use as many in this sauce as you'd like. If you want to save some for later, arrange them on a baking sheet lined with parchment paper, and freeze. Once frozen, they can be transferred to a ziplock bag and kept frozen for up to 4 months.

Add the remaining meatballs directly to the tomato sauce. Add the ribs and the whole sausages. Add the basil and bay leaf, and braise, covered, over low heat for 2 hours, stirring occasionally. Once braised, remove the sausages and cut in thirds, then add them back to the sauce. Serve with the Slow-Cooked Polenta (page 122) or your favorite pasta, along with some freshly grated Parmigiano-Reggiano and fresh basil leaves. Leftovers can be frozen with the meat submerged in the sauce for up to 3 months.

SLOW-COOKED POLENTA WITH CHEDDAR & OLIVE OIL

SERVES 4–6

1 cup medium or coarse grind cornmeal (I prefer Bob's Red Mill; not quick-cooking)

5 cups low-sodium chicken or vegetable stock

Kosher salt

1 cup milk

3 Tbsp cold butter

¼ cup grated Parmigiano-Reggiano

¾ cup grated cheddar

Black pepper

Drizzle of olive oil

Two factors make a big difference here: the quality of your polenta (I like Bob's Red Mill medium grind cornmeal) and the time you allow it to cook down (3 hours minimum). Most of that cooking time is inactive, but you'll find that taking it the full duration results in incredibly silky-soft polenta with the lightest possible mouthfeel. The dish can be made the day before and easily reconstituted with a bit of water when you're ready to serve it, and then the whole thing gets finished with cheese and as much butter as you're comfortable consuming. The result is a super-versatile side that loves something saucy—Sunday Gravy (page 121) or Barbecue Pomegranate Short Ribs (page 209), for example—and it makes a nice, sumptuous break from rice, potatoes, or noodles.

In a medium heavy-bottomed pot, combine the cornmeal and stock, stir in a pinch of salt, and set it over the lowest possible heat setting, covered, for 3–4 hours. Every 30 or so minutes, give the bottom a stir and check the liquid level. The cornmeal will swell and absorb the liquid, but you will likely need to add more during the cooking process (you can use water for the top-ups). If it looks like it's cooking too quickly and absorbing too much liquid, add more as needed and try to keep the heat low to facilitate the long cooking, or cover it halfway with the lid. The longer and slower you cook, the lighter and creamier your final product will be.

After 3 hours, remove the lid, add the milk, and cook, uncovered, for 1 hour. This will help cook off any extra moisture. Once it has the consistency of a soft porridge (about 4 hours total), stir in the butter and cheese.

Once the polenta is done the initial cook stage, you can let it cool and hold it until you're ready to serve it: reheat over low heat with a small amount of water, stirring frequently to achieve a lush, creamy consistency.

To serve, add the cold butter, grated cheeses, and a few twists of fresh pepper, and stir vigorously until well combined, light, and fluffy. Check the seasoning and drizzle with olive oil.

TRIPLE-COOKED FRENCH FRIES

SERVES 4–6

First there were French fries. Incredible stuff. Then some Parisian multi-Michelin-star bigwig in a tall toque came up with double-cooked French fries. The world reeled. Now I bring you triple-cooked French fries. Sure, they said it couldn't be done, but here we are. Simply the finest fries known to man and something your kids will tell their friends about at school. Oh, and before you ask, quadruple-cooked French fries are just too cooked. Doesn't work.

3 large russet potatoes,
    cut into ½-inch-square sticks

Neutral oil, for frying

2 sprigs rosemary

1 Tbsp flaky salt

In a medium pot, cover the potatoes with cold, heavily salted water. Bring to a simmer and cook until the potatoes are tender, 5–8 minutes. Remove from the water and drain, then arrange on a baking sheet lined with parchment paper and place in the freezer (this will remove a lot of the moisture from the potatoes). Freeze the potatoes for 1–2 hours.

In a deep fryer or heavy-bottomed pot, heat the oil to 275°F. Fry the potatoes from frozen in batches until lightly golden and slightly puffed, 5–8 minutes. Remove from the oil and drain, then freeze again. Once they have frozen through completely, they can be stored in an airtight container in the freezer for up to 1 month.

For the final fry, heat the oil to 375°F and fry until dark golden brown, 5–7 minutes. When the fries are almost done, in the last minute of frying, throw in the rosemary sprigs. Transfer the fries and rosemary directly to a bowl lined with paper towel to absorb some of the oil, then season generously with salt and give it all a shake to remove the rosemary leaves from the stems. Serve with aioli, ketchup, or your desired condiment.

CHOCOLATE SORBET

MAKES ABOUT 3 CUPS

You know who loves chocolate sorbet? Everyone. Everyone loves chocolate sorbet, and knowing how to make a great one literally improves a person's quality of life.

2¼ cups water, divided

1 cup sugar

¾ cup cocoa powder

6 oz 70% dark chocolate, finely chopped

1 tsp vanilla extract

1 tsp sea salt + extra for garnish

In a medium saucepan over medium-high heat, combine 1½ cups water, the sugar, and the cocoa powder. Bring to a boil and let it boil for 1 minute, whisking constantly. Remove from the heat and stir in the chopped chocolate, whisking until the chocolate has melted. Add the remaining ¾ cup water water, vanilla, and salt. Chill the mixture completely, then freeze it in your ice cream maker according to the manufacturer's instructions. Garnish with sea salt.

LEMON & SOUR CREAM ICE CREAM

MAKES ABOUT 4 CUPS

The combination of heavy cream and sour cream in this recipe completely maxes out the creaminess of this super-rich, no-holds-barred ice cream. My thinking is if you're going to go to the trouble of making your own ice cream (it's really not that much trouble), then really go for it.

1½ cups heavy cream

1 vanilla bean, split and scraped lengthwise, or 2 tsp vanilla extract

¾ cup sugar

½ cup milk

6 egg yolks

⅛ tsp kosher salt

1½ cups full-fat sour cream

1 Tbsp freshly squeezed lemon juice

In a large saucepan over medium heat, heat the heavy cream and vanilla bean seeds and pod (if using) until the cream just starts to simmer, about 10 minutes. Remove from the heat, cover, and let steep for 30 minutes.

While the cream is steeping, in a medium bowl, combine the sugar, milk, egg yolks, salt, and vanilla extract (if using that). Whisk well and set aside.

When the cream is ready, squeeze out any remaining seeds or cream from the pod, then discard the pod. Add the egg mixture to the saucepan and whisk to blend with the cream.

Cook the mixture over medium-low heat, stirring with a silicone spatula and constantly sweeping the bottom and sides of the pan to avoid scorching. When the mixture coats the back of the spatula, scrape the mixture into a strainer set over a large bowl. Allow the mixture to cool completely, then whisk in the sour cream. Refrigerate overnight.

Before freezing, stir in the lemon juice. Freeze in an ice cream maker according to the manufacturer's instructions. Immediately transfer the churned ice cream to a covered container and store in the freezer until serving.

CINNAMON BUTTERMILK ICE CREAM

MAKES ABOUT 3 CUPS

1½ cups heavy cream

¾ cup sugar, divided

1 Tbsp cinnamon

½ vanilla bean, split and
    scraped lengthwise,
    or 1 tsp vanilla extract

5 egg yolks

1 cup buttermilk

Pinch kosher salt

Buttermilk gets a bad rap. Admittedly, on its own, it's kind of hard to take and you certainly wouldn't want to sit down with a big warm glass of it, but in a situation like this, the milk's rich, tangy flavor adds complexity and creaminess to this cinnamon-spiked vanilla ice cream. This goes well with any pie, tart, or cake, but particularly the Rhubarb Custard Pie (page 96) and the Upside-Down Poached-Pear Cake (page 164).

In a large heavy-bottomed saucepan, combine the cream, half of the sugar, the cinnamon, and the vanilla bean seeds and pod (if using) and bring to a simmer over medium heat.

In a large bowl, whisk the egg yolks with the remaining sugar.

Remove the cream mixture from the heat and slowly drizzle a small amount into the yolk mixture, whisking constantly to keep the eggs from curdling. Do this a few more times to warm up the yolks before pouring the yolk mixture back into the cream, still whisking constantly.

Cook the cream mixture over low heat until it's thick enough to coat the back of a spoon. Strain the cream mixture and whisk in the buttermilk, vanilla extract (if using that), and salt. Cool completely, then freeze it in your ice cream maker according to the manufacturer's directions.

UPSIDE-DOWN POACHED PEAR CAKE

ALMOND APPLE CAKE

MAKES ONE 10-INCH TART
OR CAKE

Crumbly and tender, this cake has a terrific rich nuttiness, thanks to both the sliced almonds and the use of almond flour, that feels perfectly suited to home cooking. Granny Smiths, with their natural tartness and firm texture, shine in this kind of preparation, but Pink Ladies would also be a good choice.

⅔ cup butter

¼ cup honey

1 cup all-purpose flour

1 cup almond flour

½ cup sugar

2 tsp baking powder

¼ tsp kosher salt

⅔ cup plain, full-fat yogurt
   + extra for serving

2 tsp vanilla extract

2 Granny Smith apples,
   peeled and ¼-inch diced

¼ cup sliced almonds, toasted

2 Tbsp pearl sugar

Preheat the oven to 350°F. Butter or spray a 10-inch tart pan or springform. Set aside.

In a small saucepan, combine the butter and honey. Cook over medium heat until the honey has liquefied and the butter has melted. Set aside to cool.

In a medium bowl, combine both flours, sugar, baking powder, and salt.

In a large bowl, combine the yogurt with the honey-butter mixture. Add the vanilla and stir to combine. Add in the dry ingredients and stir until just combined, being careful not to overmix.

Spread the batter in the pan and top with diced apples, sliced almonds, and pearl sugar. Bake for about 45 minutes, until golden brown on top and a tester inserted into the center comes out clean. Serve with extra yogurt on top.

CHOCOLATE COCONUT SAND CAKE

MAKES ONE 10-INCH CAKE

I don't know why sand cakes aren't more popular. They've been around forever, but don't seem to be served in very many places. Maybe it's the name. To be clear, there is no sand in the recipe. What I like about them is they combine the lightness of a sponge cake with the heft of a butter cake. Anyway, I think once you try this one, your family will insist that you make it all the time, and maybe that way we can get sand cakes back in favor.

1 cup coconut oil + 1 tsp for greasing, room temperature

¼ cup unsweetened desiccated coconut

1½ cups arrowroot starch

3 eggs

1 cup sugar

3 Tbsp Grand Marnier

1 tsp vanilla extract

⅓ cup cocoa powder

2 tsp baking powder

¼ tsp kosher salt

⅓ cup freeze-dried raspberry powder (see tip)

Preheat the oven to 350°F. Grease a 10-inch Bundt pan with 1 tsp coconut oil, then coat with the shredded coconut. Set aside.

In the bowl of a stand mixer fitted with the paddle attachment, or in a large bowl with a hand mixer, combine the remaining 1 cup coconut oil and the arrowroot starch. Beat until the oil is completely incorporated into the starch and no lumps remain.

In a separate bowl, whisk the eggs and sugar until light and fluffy, then add the Grand Marnier, vanilla, cocoa powder, baking powder, and salt. Little by little, add the egg mixture into the coconut oil mixture, beating until light and smooth. Scrape the batter into the prepared cake pan and smooth out the top.

Bake for 40 minutes, or until a cake tester inserted into the center comes out clean. Turn the cake out of the pan and cool completely on a wire rack. Using a small, fine-mesh sieve, generously dust the cake with the raspberry powder as you would with icing sugar. To serve, transfer the cake to a cake plate or stand. I like to serve this with some cold cream poured overtop. Store under a domed cake lid or a bowl turned upside down. It'll last at room temperature for a few days.

KITCHEN TIP: If you can't find freeze-dried raspberry powder, you can buy dried raspberries and blitz them in a blender to get a powder consistency.

MEYER LEMON RICOTTA COOKIES

MAKES ABOUT 2 DOZEN COOKIES

A Meyer lemon is a hybrid citrus creation that's a cross between a citron—the ur-citrus—a mandarin, and a pomelo. Think of it as a lemon with the full-features package. Here, I'm using the juice and the zest to take these pillowy little lemon cookies somewhere very special.

1¼ cups all-purpose flour

1 tsp baking powder

½ tsp fine sea salt

¼ cup softened unsalted butter

¾ cup sugar

1 egg, room temperature

1 cup full-fat dry ricotta (see tip)

3 Tbsp honey

½ tsp vanilla extract

Zest and juice of 1 Meyer lemon

GLAZE

1 cup icing sugar

Zest and juice of 2 Meyer lemons

In a bowl, mix together the flour, baking powder, and sea salt, and set aside. In a large bowl, combine the butter and sugar and beat with a hand mixer until light and fluffy, about 2–3 minutes. Add the egg and mix until well blended. Add the ricotta, honey, vanilla, lemon zest, and lemon juice and mix until well blended.

Add in the flour mixture and beat just to incorporate. Be careful not to overmix. Cover the batter with plastic wrap and chill in the fridge for at least 1 hour, and up to 4 hours, before baking.

Preheat the oven to 375°F and line two baking sheets with parchment paper.

Once the dough has hydrated, place heaping tablespoons of it on the lined baking sheets, about 1½ inches apart. Bake for 15 minutes, until the cookies are firm and set but have not yet begun to brown on the edges. Allow the cookies to cool for 15 minutes on a wire rack, or until cool to the touch. If you want to bake the full batch at once, make sure to rotate the baking sheets halfway through; otherwise, feel free to bake in batches.

In a small bowl, mix the icing sugar, lemon zest, and lemon juice until well blended and glossy. Using a tablespoon, spoon the glaze onto a cooled cookie and spread it around using the bowl of the spoon. Repeat with the remaining cookies. Allow the glaze to dry for about 30 minutes. Eat the cookies immediately or store for up to 2 days in an airtight container.

KITCHEN TIP: If the ricotta has liquid with it, strain the ricotta to get rid of excess liquid. The drier the ricotta, the better.

HOLIDAYS & SPECIAL OCCASIONS

"IF YOU REALLY WANT TO MAKE A FRIEND, GO TO SOMEONE'S HOUSE AND EAT WITH HIM. . . . THE PEOPLE WHO GIVE YOU THEIR FOOD GIVE YOU THEIR HEART."

—CESAR CHAVEZ

We know that any self-respecting dad would happily take on a 12-course holiday blowout single-handedly if the need arose—and nail each component—but for the most part, we prefer to think of holiday feasts as more of a team effort. This collection of recipes has you covered no matter what course you're called upon to crush.

Don't hold off on these recipes just for Labor Day either. If you feel like celebrating Respect for the Aged Day (third Monday in September), National Hairball Awareness Day (last Friday in April), or World Sword Swallowers Day (last Saturday in February), get cooking.

It's probably fair to say that these aren't "traditional" holiday recipes, as there aren't any for stuffed turkeys or marshmallow-topped casseroles. Think of these as the kinds of recipes that would sit well on a holiday table or enliven a celebratory occasion. None of them is particularly challenging, and you are, of course, cordially invited to throw any of them down whenever the urge strikes.

FRIED GREEN TOMATOES WITH AVOCADO RANCH DRESSING

SERVES 4

Fried green tomatoes are everyone's favorite summer dish, even if they don't know it yet. If you have a garden, or even grow a few tomato plants—and you really should—you know that feeling of wanting to harvest those plants ASAP, and this is a satisfying way to do that. Also, if you've got any tomatoes that have fallen off the vine, this is a great way to use them up. As well, green tomatoes are starting to show up more often on grocery store shelves in season. Tomatoes and basil get all the attention, but this recipe proves that tomatoes and dill are every bit as great a combination.

3 or 4 large firm green tomatoes

3 eggs

½ cup milk

¾ cup all-purpose flour

2 tsp kosher salt

Black pepper

Pinch cayenne

⅓ cup fine breadcrumbs

⅓ cup fine cornmeal

Vegetable oil, for shallow frying

¾ cup Buttermilk Avocado Ranch (page 225)

Flaky salt, for garnish

2 sprigs dill, picked, for garnish

Core and slice the tomatoes ⅓ inch thick, discarding just the end pieces, as the breading will not stick to the skins.

Set up three large bowls. Mix the eggs and milk together in one bowl until well combined.

In the second, mix the flour with salt, pepper, and cayenne. In the third bowl, mix the breadcrumbs and cornmeal.

Working with only a couple of slices at a time so as not to overcrowd the bowl, dip the tomatoes in the flour mixture, shaking off any excess, and then into the egg mixture. Finally, firmly press both sides of the tomato into the breadcrumb mixture. Place the tomatoes in a single layer on a baking sheet. Continue until all the tomatoes are breaded.

In a large cast-iron pan set over medium heat, heat ½ inch of vegetable oil. Place the tomatoes in the frying pan in batches of four, being careful not to overcrowd the pan. Cook the tomatoes for about 2 minutes on each side, until golden brown. Transfer the fried tomatoes to paper towel to drain and repeat until done.

Arrange the tomatoes on a platter and garnish with the avocado ranch, flaky salt, and picked dill.

ENDIVE SALAD WITH GOUDA, TOASTED WALNUTS & PARSLEY

SERVES 4

Here we're taking a classic salad starring endive and employing it as a vehicle for a dressing built around apples and shallots. The meaty texture of endive is by far my favorite for a crisp salad. You've got these fresh, crispy greens, your sweet-and-sour vinaigrette, your silky cheese on top, and crunchy nuts. We're using Gouda and walnuts in this version, but because this recipe is all about learning to properly balance a salad, once you've got it under your belt, you can play around with just about any hard cheese and different nuts.

1 cup coarsely chopped walnuts

½ tsp kosher salt

¼ tsp pepper

1 Tbsp maple syrup

1 Tbsp olive oil

3½ oz wedge Gouda

1 head white radicchio, quartered and core removed

1 head Treviso, quartered and core removed

2 heads Belgian endive, quartered and core removed

1 cup picked parsley leaves

Apple, Thyme & Shallot Vinaigrette (page 224)

½ green apple, finely sliced

Preheat the oven to 350°F.

In a small bowl, combine the walnuts, salt, pepper, maple syrup, and olive oil. Bake on a baking sheet for 20 minutes, or until golden brown.

Using a vegetable peeler, a mandoline, or the slicing blade on your box grater, slice the Gouda into thin ribbons.

Tear or slice the radicchio and Treviso into manageable pieces. Toss the endive and parsley leaves with a few tablespoons of the vinaigrette. Build a nice base on your serving platter using the different lettuces, then garnish with the sliced apple, Gouda, spiced walnuts, and a generous pour of vinaigrette.

YOGURT-BAKED COD WITH WALNUTS, TARRAGON & DILL

SERVES 4

The combination of yogurt and fish sounds a bit unusual at first, until you think of all the great dishes where fish is paired with cream. That's the tradition we're building on here. This recipe is highly amenable to being sized up or down depending on how many people you need to feed, so it works as well for a date night as it does for a dinner party. Kids seem to respond to this dish as well. Maybe it's the crunch from the butter-toasted walnuts or the creamy tanginess of the yogurt, or the floral herbaceousness of the tarragon (an underrated herb), but this dish is a hit even with picky eaters. This was inspired by a Stuart Cameron recipe that I love.

Olive oil

Four thick 5 oz fillets skinless, boneless wild-caught cod

Kosher salt and black pepper

1 shallot, minced

Zest and juice of 1 lemon, divided

2 tsp finely chopped chives

¾ cup plain, full-fat yogurt

¼ cup dry white wine

1 egg, beaten

3 Tbsp butter

⅓ cup coarsely chopped walnuts

2 slices bread, crusts removed and finely diced

Pinch flaky salt

2 sprigs tarragon, picked

2 sprigs dill, picked

Preheat the oven to 400°F.

Heat a cast-iron pan over medium-high heat until quite hot. Add enough olive oil to coat the bottom. Lightly season one side of the cod fillets with a pinch of salt and pepper. In batches, sear the cod on one side until just browned, about 2 minutes. Remove and repeat with the remaining fish. Rinse the pan to cool and remove any excess oil.

In a medium bowl, combine the shallots, lemon juice, and chives. Season with salt and pepper. Add the yogurt, wine, and egg and mix well until fully combined. Spread the yogurt sauce over the bottom of the cast-iron pan or a casserole dish, then place the fish on top, seared side up. Bake the fish until the sauce has set and the fish has cooked through, about 20 minutes.

As the fish bakes, melt the butter in a nonstick pan set over medium heat. Add the walnuts and breadcrumbs and toast, stirring, until the nuts are golden brown, about 5 minutes. Set aside to cool. Once the walnuts have cooled, add the lemon zest, flaky salt, tarragon, and dill. Sprinkle the mixture on top of the fish, and serve immediately.

ONE-POT SHELLFISH BOIL

SERVES 6–8

The Lowcountry's answer to bouillabaisse combines all of the delicious joy of that French classic with none of the fussy, rule-bound dogma. Pick up a whack of good-quality shellfish, toss it in a pot with some aromatics and smoky sausage and you're off to the races.

12 oz dry white wine

2 white onions, quartered

1 lb mini red potatoes

4 cups water

1 bulb fennel, fronds trimmed and cut into eighths

½ head garlic

5 sprigs thyme

5 sprigs parsley

Pinch chili flakes

1 pint cherry tomatoes

1 Tbsp Old Bay Seasoning

2 bay leaves

1 leek, white and light green parts only, washed and sliced into rounds

2 ears corn, husked and cut into 2-inch rounds

One 1½ lb live lobster

½ lb smoked sausage, like kielbasa or andouille

1½ lb littleneck clams, soaked and scrubbed of sand

8 large prawns in shell

1 lb mussels, cleaned and debearded

Kosher salt

Crusty bread and good butter, for serving

1 lemon, cut into wedges

In a large pot, combine the white wine, onions, potatoes, and water and bring to a boil over high heat for 7 minutes, to soften the potatoes. Add the fennel, garlic, thyme, parsley, chili flakes, tomatoes, Old Bay Seasoning, bay leaves, leeks, and corn and return to high heat.

The second stage is all about timing the protein: add the whole lobster, fully submerged in the boiling broth, cover with a lid for 4 minutes, and cook on high heat. Next, add the sausage and clams, replace the lid, and boil for 3 more minutes. Finally, add the prawns and mussels and cook for a final 3 minutes, or until both the clams and mussels are wide open (discard any that don't open after this time).

Check the broth for seasoning and add salt or more Old Bay if you like. Serve straight from the pot with crusty bread and butter and lemon wedges.

ROAST CHICKEN OVER POMMES BOULANGÈRE

SERVES 4

None of the great French chefs of the world would consider this a true, classic pommes boulangère, but that's where the inspiration comes from. What makes this recipe especially exciting is that as the potatoes cook, they soak up all the luscious fat and flavor from the chicken dripping down into them. Also, the chicken will be done slightly before the potatoes, so it forces you to let the bird rest (always a good habit to get into) before you carve it. The result is a beautifully roasted chicken and a batch of incredible potatoes with a crisp, dark exterior and a luscious, almost molten, interior. All that for what is probably 20 minutes of prep time, all of which can be done ahead, so you just need to throw it in the oven when you're ready to eat.

One 3 lb chicken

5 Tbsp butter, softened, divided

3 sprigs rosemary, divided

2½ tsp kosher salt, divided

½ tsp cracked pepper

1 tsp sugar

4 medium Yukon Gold potatoes

2 shallots, thinly sliced

3 cloves garlic, crushed

2 oz (about ⅓ cup) diced pancetta

4 sprigs thyme

3 slices lemon

Using a paper towel, pat the chicken dry. Using your fingers, gently separate the skin from the breast of the chicken. Smear 3 Tbsp softened butter under the skin. Truss the legs of the chicken—there are some great YouTube videos showing how to do this, and it's easiest to understand by watching.

Pick 1 sprig of rosemary and finely chop the leaves. Mix the chopped rosemary with 2 tsp salt, and the pepper and sugar. Distribute this seasoning evenly over the interior and exterior of the chicken. Set the chicken in the fridge, uncovered, for a minimum of 30 minutes or up to overnight.

Preheat the oven to 400°F.

Grease a medium casserole dish with 1 Tbsp butter. Slice the potatoes into thin rounds, then arrange in concentric circles in the bottom of the casserole dish. Dot the potatoes with the remaining 1 Tbsp butter, then place the shallots, garlic, pancetta, remaining 2 sprigs rosemary, thyme sprigs, and lemon slices, along with the remaining ½ tsp salt overtop.

Place the prepared chicken on top of the potatoes. Roast in the oven until the juices run clear and a thermometer inserted between the thigh and breast reads 165°F. Remove the chicken from the casserole dish and place on a wire rack set over a baking sheet to rest and circulate the air (this will help avoid soggy skin). Return the casserole dish with the potatoes to the oven for 15 minutes to allow the aromatics and potatoes to brown and finish cooking. When the chicken is sufficiently rested, cut into quarters and serve overtop some potatoes.

FLOCK SPICED CHICKEN, CHICKPEAS, BITTER GREENS & MINI POTATOES

SERVES 8–10

As far as I'm concerned, there's nothing more seductive than a perfectly roasted chicken. This recipe, despite being a quintessential 5-minute-prep, one-pot dish, elevates roast chicken for home cooking in a way that you never could pull off in a restaurant. Don't tell anyone, but this is one of those dishes that looks and eats like it is much more labor-intensive than it is. It is impressive enough to serve at an entertaining event, but also simple enough to put together for a weeknight. Chickpeas pop up a lot in my cooking given that they're a cheap and accessible ingredient with great health benefits. If you like, you can halve the ingredients to serve fewer people.

CHICKEN

Two 3 lb whole chickens

¼ cup Flock Chicken Dry Rub (page 228)

VEGETABLES

3 cups mini potatoes, skin on, larger ones cut in half

1 Spanish onion, cut in wedges

¼ cup olive oil, divided

Kosher salt and black pepper

2 bunches rapini, stems trimmed

4 cloves garlic, crushed

2 lemons, cut in half

2 cups canned chickpeas, rinsed and drained

½ cup golden raisins

8 sprigs thyme

4 sprigs rosemary

KITCHEN TIP: Brining your chicken will bring your meal to the next level. I prefer dry curing to wet brining because I think it gives the chicken a much more appealing texture. Wet brines can result in a rubbery, ham-like texture if your timing isn't just right.

Liberally dust the chickens inside and out with the dry rub, making sure all crevices are well spiced. Shake off any excess.

Using butcher's twine, tie the legs tightly together, then pull the string around to the front of the breast. Tie a knot just under the wishbone, holding the chicken tightly together. There are some great videos online that show you how to truss chicken as well. Place the chickens on a baking sheet and loosely cover with plastic wrap. Refrigerate overnight or for up to 24 hours.

Arrange a rack in the center of the oven and preheat the oven to 400°F. Place the potatoes and onions into a roasting dish large enough to hold both chickens with extra space. Drizzle the potatoes and onions with 2 Tbsp olive oil and season with salt and pepper. Toss to coat. Place the chickens on top of the vegetables. Bake, uncovered, for 30 minutes.

Remove the roasting pan from the oven and carefully lift up the chickens and transfer them to a plate. Add the rapini, garlic, lemons, chickpeas, raisins, thyme, and rosemary to the pan, and mix in with the potatoes and onions. Smooth out into an even layer. Season with salt and pepper. Put the chickens back on top of all the vegetables and return to the oven.

Bake, uncovered, for 40 minutes, or until a thermometer inserted between the thigh and leg reads 165°F. Remove the roasting pan from the oven and let the chickens rest over the vegetables for 15 minutes, loosely covered with aluminum foil. Portion the chicken into pieces and serve on platters family-style.

WARM POTATO SALAD

SERVES 4–6

This hearty salad makes great use of the Crispy Pancetta & Shallot Vinaigrette that also shows up in the Warm Beet Salad (page 171). The key is to hit the potatoes with the vinaigrette while they're still hot. That way, the vegetables are porous and they soak up the dressing like a sponge. Try to keep that in mind anytime you're dressing warm ingredients with a vinaigrette. This salad, alongside a nice piece of grilled meat or fish or simply some grilled asparagus, is a pretty dreamy combination.

2 cups baby potatoes

½ batch Crispy Pancetta & Shallot Vinaigrette (page 224)

3 eggs

Kosher salt and black pepper, to taste

¼ cup picked and torn parsley leaves

In a medium pot, cover the potatoes in cold salted water. Bring to a boil over medium-high heat and cook until tender, about 12 minutes. Remove from the water (keeping the cooking water still in the pot) and gently smash them while still warm. Dress in the pancetta vinaigrette, reserving 2 Tbsp. Place the potatoes on a serving plate.

In the potato water, boil the eggs until jammy, about 8 minutes. Peel and quarter the eggs, dress with salt, pepper, parsley, and the remaining vinaigrette, and place overtop the potatoes. Serve warm.

BRAISED LAMB SHANK SOUP WITH LENTILS, FETA & FAVA BEANS

SERVES 6

This recipe has been a staple of mine both in restaurants and at home. The flavor starts at the base, so the magic is in taking your time to properly sear the lamb shanks, cook your aromatics gently and carefully, and draw as much flavor from the cinnamon, star anise, thyme, and red wine to add to its success. If you can use the red wine you're drinking for dinner—a big shiraz, say—in the braise, so much the better. This is the ultimate winter dish, but if you want to take it in a spring direction, simply replace the lentils with fava beans and peas. Like most braises and stews, this keeps in the fridge and freezes really well, so it's worth making a big pot and then portioning it off and keeping the leftovers in the freezer.

2 Tbsp canola oil

3 lamb shanks

Kosher salt and black pepper

3 carrots, cut into 1-inch pieces

3 celery ribs, cut into 1-inch pieces

1 small yellow onion, cut into 1-inch pieces

½ cup tomato paste

1 cup dry red wine

1 cinnamon stick

1 bay leaf

2 sprigs rosemary

2 pieces star anise

3 garlic cloves, chopped

Peel of ½ lemon

3 cups chicken stock

1 batch lentils (see recipe on page 79)

2 lb fresh fava beans in pod or 1 cup frozen blanched fava beans

3 Tbsp Toasted Sourdough Breadcrumbs with Rosemary & Sea Salt (page 228; optional)

½ cup crumbled feta

Heat the canola oil in a heavy large soup pot over medium heat. Season the lamb shanks with salt and pepper and add them to the pot. Brown on all sides, 5–7 minutes. Transfer the lamb to a clean plate and set aside.

Add the carrots, celery, and onions and cook, stirring, for 3–5 minutes, until translucent. Add the tomato paste, stir to coat the vegetables, and continue cooking for 3 minutes. We are just looking to cook out the raw tomato flavor and add another depth of sweetness by slightly caramelizing the sugars. Add the red wine and reduce by half. Add the cinnamon stick, bay leaf, rosemary, star anise, garlic, lemon peel, and chicken stock, and season well with salt and pepper. Place the browned lamb shanks in the pot, cover, and cook over low heat for about 3 hours, or until the meat is falling off the bone, turning the lamb shanks over halfway.

Carefully remove the lamb shanks from the pot and set aside. Strain the braising liquid, making sure to press down on the vegetables going through the strainer to squeeze every last drop of flavor from them. Pick out any pieces of meat that have fallen off the bone, and set aside with the lamb shanks. Discard the vegetables and skim the excess fat from the stock. Return the skimmed stock to the pot.

Separate the lamb meat from the bones, picking out and discarding any large pieces of fat and tissue. Cut the meat into bite-sized pieces and add them back into the pot.

While the soup simmers, prepare the fava beans. Bring a medium pot of salted water to a boil on high heat and prepare an ice bath with tap water and ice. Split the fava bean pods to remove the beans. Add the fava beans to the boiling water and cook for just 1 minute, then immediately transfer them to the ice bath. Once cool, strain the beans and peel off the shells, collecting the beans in a small bowl as you go.

To assemble the dish, stir in the cooked lentils and fava beans into the soup. Check for seasoning and serve with the toasted sourdough breadcrumbs and crumbled feta.

ROASTED BABY ROOT VEGETABLES WITH BEET HUMMUS & CASHEW DUKKAH

SERVES 4–6

4 small carrots, scrubbed

4 whole baby beets, scrubbed

4 radishes, scrubbed

4 baby turnips

4 small Jerusalem artichokes, scrubbed

2 cloves garlic, skin on, crushed

1 shallot, halved

4 sprigs thyme

1 Tbsp maple syrup

2 Tbsp olive oil

1½ tsp kosher salt

1 tsp black pepper

1 cup Roasted Beet Hummus (page 229)

2 Tbsp Cashew Dukkah (page 228)

Serve this versatile salad as a substantial lunch on its own or alongside a wide range of meals, especially the Braised Lamb Shank Soup (page 152) or Yogurt-Baked Cod (page 142). We're taking a hands-off approach with this dish and just scrubbing up our root vegetables and tossing them in the oven. We're looking for a rustic finish here, heavily roasted with crispy, brown frizzled ends on the carrots and a kind of leathery look to the beets and radishes. The only thing to look out for is that you want your vegetables to cook at roughly the same speed, so if you've got giant carrots and baby beets, cut the carrots down to size. If you don't have the cashew dukkah handy, feel free to drizzle some yogurt or crumble some creamy Macedonian feta overtop.

Preheat the oven to 400°F. Remove the leafy tops of the carrots, beets, radishes, and turnips.

If the vegetables are roughly the same size, they can be left whole. If not, they can be minimally cut to about the same size to ensure even cooking. In a large bowl, combine everything except the beet hummus and cashew dukkah and toss until the vegetables are well coated. Arrange in an even layer on a baking sheet. Roast for about 50 minutes, until fully softened and caramelized, turning once.

Spread the beet hummus evenly over the bottom of a large plate or platter. Arrange the roasted vegetables overtop, and garnish generously with cashew dukkah. Serve warm.

CAST-IRON BAKED DELICATA SQUASH GRATIN

SERVES 6

Like a Norman Rockwell painting come to life, this warm take on a satisfying gratin is kind of like a modernized scalloped potato dish, just a little lighter and a little healthier. It looks impressive and people flip out when they see it, but all the work is just in the assembly; after that, you can just set it in the oven and forget about it. I also love that the cast-iron pan cooks the squash and acts as the serving vessel, meaning there's one less dish to clean up after dinner. To save time, you could easily par-bake it 1 day ahead, then top it with the gratin and finish it with a final blast in the oven on the day of.

2 large delicata squash

2 Tbsp vegetable oil

2 tsp sea salt

Black pepper

3½ oz wedge Brie, thinly sliced

3 cloves garlic, smashed

½ bunch thyme

5 sprigs rosemary

1 large shallot, sliced into rounds

¼ lb butter, cut into small cubes

½ cup Toasted Sourdough Breadcrumbs with Rosemary & Sea Salt (page 228)

½ cup grated white cheddar

⅓ cup skinned hazelnuts, toasted and cracked

2 Tbsp melted butter, cooled

Preheat the oven to 375°F.

Cut the delicata squash in half horizontally, and use a spoon to scoop out the seeds. Cut the squash into ¼-inch rings. In a bowl, toss the sliced squash with vegetable oil, salt, and a couple twists of fresh pepper. Arrange the squash in a cast-iron pan with the slices standing up straight and packed in tightly, interspersing some Brie slices in throughout.

Place the garlic, thyme, rosemary, and shallots overtop the squash and Brie. Scatter the cubes of butter evenly overtop.

Bake the squash for about 30 minutes, or until tender and lightly browned.

Meanwhile, in a bowl, mix the toasted sourdough breadcrumbs, cheddar, hazelnuts, and melted butter.

Evenly distribute the breadcrumb and cheese mixture overtop the squash and bake for a further 15 minutes, or until browned and golden. Serve straight from the pan.

KITCHEN TIP: This winter dish works well with just about any root vegetable you like, including celery root, beets, and sweet potatoes.

ROASTED SQUASH & MINI POTATOES WITH SAGE & WHOLE GARLIC

SERVES 6

I come back to this hearty roast again and again through fall, through winter, and into early spring. I'm partial to delicata or buttercup squash—something thin-skinned—for this preparation because they taste great and I love the way they look with the skin on. It also saves you the hassle of peeling. This is great for a dinner party because it's visually appealing and it's another low-prep, high-impact dish.

1 delicata squash, cut into ½-inch rings, seeds removed

1 acorn squash, cut into 2-inch wedges, seeds removed

2 cups mini creamer potatoes

2 leeks, white part only, washed well and cut into ½-inch slices

1 head garlic, split horizontally

½ cup packed sage leaves

½ cup raw pumpkin seeds

6 sprigs thyme

2 Tbsp maple syrup

2 Tbsp red wine vinegar

2 tsp kosher salt

Black pepper

Preheat the oven to 375°F and line a baking sheet with parchment paper.

Toss all the ingredients together in a bowl, then transfer to the baking sheet, spreading them out in an even layer. Bake for 30–40 minutes, until the squashes and potatoes are nicely browned and softened throughout.

LEMON OLIVE OIL CAKE WITH RASPBERRIES

The combination of butter and olive oil gives this cake a little something special that your family might not recognize at first but will definitely have them asking for the secret. Get the kids to make the lemon sugar if they're around, and their hands will smell incredible afterward. The visual beauty of this cake derives from the bright red raspberry filling and the billowy, caramelized meringue top. That top, incidentally, is the one place in this recipe where you really have to pay attention. It will go from perfectly caramelized to utterly carbonized in a minute if you're not paying attention. Anyway, if that happens, scrape it off and enjoy your still-delicious cake.

MAKES ONE 10-INCH CAKE

1 cup + 2 Tbsp sugar, divided

Zest of 2 lemons

4 eggs, room temperature

3 Tbsp milk, room temperature

1¾ cups all-purpose flour

1½ tsp baking powder

⅔ cup extra-virgin olive oil

¼ cup melted butter

1 Tbsp freshly squeezed lemon juice (½ lemon)

1 pint fresh raspberries

2 Tbsp water

1 batch Lemon Curd (page 222)

MERINGUE

4 egg whites

3 Tbsp sugar

Preheat the oven to 350°F. Grease a 10-inch springform pan with butter, then dust with flour, tapping out any excess.

In a large bowl, combine 1 cup sugar and the lemon zest and rub them together between your fingers until the sugar is moist and fragrant. Beat the eggs into the sugar with a hand mixer until the mixture is pale and thick, about 3 minutes. Gently beat in the milk.

Sift the flour and baking powder into the batter and beat until fully incorporated, making sure not to overmix. Add the olive oil, melted butter, and lemon juice and beat until blended.

Pour the batter into the prepared pan and bake for about 35 minutes, until the cake is golden and pulling away from the sides of the pan. A tester inserted into the center should come out clean. Remove the cake from the oven and set the oven to broil.

As the cake is baking, in a small saucepan, combine the raspberries, the remaining 2 Tbsp sugar, and the water. Cook over medium heat just until the raspberries start to break apart, then remove from the heat and set aside.

For the meringue, in a large clean, dry bowl of a stand mixer, beat the egg whites on medium speed until they reach soft peaks, about 4 minutes. With the mixer still running, add the sugar slowly, 1 tsp at a time, and continue to beat until the texture reaches stiff peaks.

Let the cake cool completely before removing from the springform pan, and slicing in half horizontally to create two layers. Spoon in the raspberry mixture, making sure to leave none of the juice behind, over the cut side of one-half of the cake, and spread it out evenly. On top of the raspberries, spread a thick layer of lemon curd. Using the back of a spoon, evenly distribute the meringue over the other layer, creating an irregular but even texture. Broil this layer in the center of the oven, with the meringue facing up, until the meringue has caramelized, taking care not to let it burn. Depending on your oven, it should take about 2–3 minutes, but pay close attention.

Lay the meringue layer, with the meringue facing up, on top of the layer with the raspberries and lemon curd, then slice and serve. This cake is best served the day of, so try to make and broil the meringue just before serving.

FLOURLESS CHOCOLATE CAKE WITH CARDAMOM, CINNAMON, BLOOD ORANGES & FRESH CREAM

MAKES ONE 9-INCH CAKE

6 Tbsp butter

8 oz 70% bittersweet chocolate, finely chopped

6 eggs, separated

2 Tbsp + 1 cup heavy cream, divided

1 tsp cardamom

1 tsp cinnamon

¼ tsp kosher salt

½ cup sugar

2 blood oranges, suprèmed and juices reserved

Cardamom is such an underrated spice. It does wonders for both sweet and savory dishes and brings an intoxicating warm, herbal, citrus flavor to everything it touches. It shows up a lot in Indian dishes, especially those calling for garam masala, and, curiously, in Scandinavian sweet baked goods. Here it's put to use to give a haunting loveliness to bittersweet chocolate. The spice's inherent citrus flavors also make it the ideal thing to bring the chocolate and blood orange flavors together.

Preheat the oven to 275°F with the rack in the center. Butter the bottom and sides of a 9-inch springform pan. Set aside.

In a large heatproof bowl, combine the 6 Tbsp butter and the chocolate over a pot of simmering water, and stir until completely melted. Set aside to cool slightly but keep warm. In a separate bowl, whisk together the egg yolks, 2 Tbsp heavy cream, cardamom, cinnamon, and salt, then whisk the egg mixture into the chocolate mixture.

In a large clean, dry bowl of a stand mixer, beat the egg whites on medium speed until they reach soft peaks, about 4 minutes. Gradually add the sugar, a few teaspoons at a time, and continue beating until glossy, stiff peaks form.

Whisk one-quarter of the egg whites into the chocolate mixture, then gently but quickly fold in the remaining egg whites. Pour the batter into the prepared pan and smooth the top with a spatula.

Bake until the cake pulls away from the sides of the pan and is set in the center, 45–50 minutes. Cool completely on a wire rack, then remove from the pan.

While the cake is baking, in a clean bowl, whip the remaining 1 cup heavy cream until it reaches soft peaks. Serve the cake at room temperature with a dollop of whipped cream and a spoonful of orange segments.

KITCHEN TIP: Whisking a portion of the egg whites into the chocolate mixture before folding in the remainder helps to lighten and balance the texture of the chocolate mixture so it comes together more evenly.

UPSIDE-DOWN POACHED-PEAR CAKE

MAKES ONE 9-INCH CAKE

There are a few steps involved in this recipe, it's true, but there's nothing especially challenging about any particular one, and the results are seriously impressive. Take a minute to make sure the pears are tightly and neatly packed into the pan when assembling the cake; this will help build that beautiful, burnished caramel layer and make for the most dramatic presentation possible.

POACHED PEARS

2 cups dry red wine

½ cup sugar

4 Bosc pears, peeled and halved, cores removed with a melon baller

2 Tbsp freshly squeezed lemon juice

3 sprigs thyme

1 cinnamon stick

1 whole clove

STEAMED PUDDING BATTER

3 eggs, separated

1 cup sugar, divided

3 Tbsp canola oil

1 cup milk

Zest and juice of 2 lemons (about 2 Tbsp zest and ¼ cup juice)

1 cup pastry flour

Pinch kosher salt

To poach the pears, in a medium saucepan set over medium heat, heat the wine and sugar until the sugar is dissolved. Add the pears, lemon juice, thyme, cinnamon stick, and clove, making sure there's enough liquid to cover the pears. If not, add enough water to cover. Reduce the heat to medium-low and simmer, covered, for 20–25 minutes, until the pears are tender. Lift the pears into a bowl using a slotted spoon. Once the pears are cool enough to handle, cut them once more so they are in quarters. Pour the poaching liquid through a strainer, then return it to the pot.

Increase the heat to high and bring the strained poaching liquid to a boil. Cook until the liquid is reduced to about ½ cup. Remove from the heat and return the pears to the liquid. Allow to cool to room temperature.

To make the batter, arrange a rack in the center of the oven and preheat to 300°F.

Butter a 9-inch cake pan (with sides at least 2 inches high) and line the bottom with parchment paper.

In a large clean, dry bowl of a stand mixer, beat the egg whites on medium speed until they reach soft peaks, about 4 minutes. With the mixer still running, stream in half of the sugar and continue whipping until stiff, glossy peaks form, about 2 more minutes. Transfer the whites to a large mixing bowl.

Clean out the bowl of the stand mixer and whip the egg yolks with the remaining sugar on medium-high until light and fluffy, about 2 minutes. Beat in the oil, milk, lemon zest and juice, flour, and salt, along with half of the whipped egg whites, just until combined. Fold in the remaining whipped egg whites with a wooden spoon.

In the prepared cake pan, neatly arrange the poached-pear quarters in a circular pattern, fitting them as tightly as possible and slightly overlapping. Pour two-thirds of the residual poaching liquid overtop the pears, reserving the rest. Gently pour the batter evenly into the pan. Spray a piece of aluminum foil with cooking spray and cover the pan with foil (spray side down).

Bake for 50 minutes to 1 hour. To test the cake, peel the foil back and check the middle of the cake with a small knife—the batter should be just cooked on top and slightly moist in the middle. Remove the cake from the oven and remove the foil. Let the cake cool for 20 minutes, then serve warm with a scoop of Cinnamon Buttermilk Ice Cream (page 126) and the reserved poaching liquid.

CRIPSY MUSHROOM, BURRATA & RADICCHIO SALAD

"THERE IS NO MORE SINCERE LOVE THAN THE LOVE OF FOOD."

—GEORGE BERNARD SHAW

Tonight's the night. Maybe the kids are at their grandparents or away at camp, or you simply fed them early and packed them off to sleep—whatever the reason, we're lighting the candles, busting out the Barry White, and opening up a bottle of something special.

Intimate dinners require a particular approach to the menu. You want it to be delicate, but also sexy; rich without overwhelming the palate. A certain lavishness is expected, but without falling into gluttony. You want to still be fresh and vibrant at the end, not inundated and overfed. When appropriate, it's nice if there are things you can cook together as a couple.

Ultimately, these are recipes you might not cook every night, but they have a certain elegance that will turn any evening into a night to remember.

Beyond just a kind of aphrodisiacal approach to feeding your significant other, we're considering "Date Night" recipes as those you cook to impress. That can include everyone from your partner to your parents or just some friends.

CRISPY MUSHROOM, BURRATA & RADICCHIO SALAD WITH HAZELNUTS & FRIED ROSEMARY

SERVES 4

10 king oyster mushrooms, cut into strips

2 handfuls Shimeji mushrooms, bases trimmed and torn into 8 clusters

4 Tbsp good-quality olive oil, divided + extra for garnish

½ shallot, sliced

4 sprigs thyme

Kosher salt and black pepper

3 sprigs rosemary

1 Tbsp butter

1 head radicchio, quartered and core removed

1 Belgian endive, quartered and core removed

2 Tbsp balsamic vinegar

4 slices sourdough

½ clove garlic

¼ cup skinned hazelnuts, toasted and cracked, divided

One 7 oz ball burrata

If you come to my house for dinner, there's a 25% chance this salad will be part of the meal. It's become a bit of a household staple. The star of the dish is not, as you might think, the burrata (in fact, it's still a substantial salad without it): it's the mushrooms that get cooked up until they're super dehydrated and crispy, almost like French fries. Basically, you can't overcook them. Like, if you think they've gone too far, you're probably getting close. They taste so good that way, especially against the bitterness of the greens, the creaminess of the burrata, and the toasted hazelnuts.

Preheat your oven to 425°F and line a baking sheet with parchment paper.

In a large bowl, toss the mushrooms, 2 Tbsp olive oil, shallot, and thyme. Transfer to the baking sheet, season with salt and pepper and roast in the oven for about 30 minutes. The mushrooms should be dark golden brown and starting to crisp around the edges.

Meanwhile, in a small pan over very low heat, combine the rosemary sprigs with the butter and remaining 2 Tbsp olive oil and fry until the rosemary sprigs are crispy and brittle, taking care not to let them burn. Remove the rosemary, lightly salt it and set aside. Reserve the oil for dressing the greens.

Slice the radicchio into ¼-inch strips and toss it together with the endive in a large bowl, then lightly dress with the reserved rosemary-scented olive oil, salt, pepper, and balsamic.

About 10 minutes prior to serving, toast the sourdough and rub with olive oil and garlic.

Transfer the greens to a large serving platter. Top with the toasted sourdough.

At this point, the mushrooms should be nearly finished, but don't rush them. Ideally, these go on the salad straight from the oven, hot and crispy. The greens can wait lightly dressed.

Pile the mushrooms in the center of the dressed greens, nice and high. Crown the mushrooms with the burrata and garnish with the fried rosemary, olive oil, a generous amount of balsamic and sea salt, and the remaining hazelnuts. Finish with a few twists of pepper overtop and another splash of olive oil, if you feel it necessary.

CREAMY FETA WITH TOASTED FENNEL SEEDS, CHILI FLAKES & DILL

SERVES 4

Having a slab of good-quality, creamy feta on hand means you're ready to whip up a quick appetizer for guests or a simple snack for yourself. There's no cooking involved beyond toasting the fennel seeds and maybe grilling some flatbread, so it comes together in no time. I think of this as a modern version of the ubiquitous baked Brie that my parents, and probably yours, served back in the day.

1 Tbsp fennel seeds

Pinch chili flakes, depending on spice tolerance

8 oz block feta

1 Tbsp honey

Handful dill sprigs

In a medium nonstick pan set over medium heat, toast the fennel seeds until lightly golden and fragrant. Add the chili flakes and lightly toast. Transfer the fennel seeds and chili flakes to a mortar and pestle and lightly crush them (kids excel at working a mortar and pestle and love to do it), or place in a clean dish towel and use the bottom of a heavy pan to crush until just broken, then sprinkle over the feta. Drizzle with honey and garnish with fresh dill sprigs. Serve with your favorite cracker or flatbread.

WARM BEET SALAD WITH PANCETTA VINAIGRETTE & TOASTED HAZELNUTS

SERVES 4

A version of this recipe has appeared in every contemporary French-inspired restaurant for about 30 years. And for good reason. The combination of sweet beets, a slightly fatty, porky vinaigrette, and carefully toasted hazelnuts is pure harmony. You could, of course, add crumbles of goat cheese if you wanted to gild the lily, but it's not required.

6 medium beets

½ batch Crispy Pancetta & Shallot Vinaigrette (page 224)

Kosher salt and black pepper

½ cup chopped toasted hazelnuts

¼ cup coarsely chopped parsley

In a large pot, cover the beets in cold water and cook over medium-high heat until tender. The timing will vary depending on the size of your beets. When the beets are cooked through, rinse them under cold water and use your fingers to remove the skins. Dry and quarter the beets. Toss the beets in the vinaigrette while still warm so they soak up the dressing like a sponge. Season with salt and pepper to taste and garnish with hazelnuts and parsley.

BURRATA SALAD WITH BUTTER LETTUCE, SWEET PEAS & PESTO VINAIGRETTE

SERVES 4

Here we're showcasing two ingredients in their prime: fresh burrata and the first peas of the season. In all the restaurants I've ever worked, the arrival of the year's first peas was always a big deal. Spring is heralded by wild leeks and asparagus, but then there's kind of a lull before the real summer harvest is in full swing. Peas bridge that gap, and they're all the more special for it. So, for me, this is kind of a quintessential early summer dish, something that takes little preparation or work and results in a truly impressive salad.

PESTO VINAIGRETTE

2 Tbsp shelled salted pistachios

2 Tbsp grated Parmigiano-Reggiano

2 ice cubes

½ cup olive oil

½ cup packed basil leaves

½ cup packed mint leaves

½ cup packed parsley leaves

½ clove garlic

½ tsp kosher salt

¼ tsp pepper

Juice of 1 lemon

SALAD

2 cups blanched and chilled sweet peas

2 heads butter lettuce, leaves separated

One 7 oz ball burrata

Kosher salt and black pepper

¼ cup packed basil leaves

¼ cup packed mint leaves

2 Tbsp shelled, toasted, crushed salted pistachios

½ lemon

Combine all the pesto vinaigrette ingredients in a blender and blend on high until just smooth, taking care not to overheat.

In a bowl, toss the peas with the pesto vinaigrette.

On a large platter, arrange the butter lettuce leaves upright so they resemble little cups. Place the burrata whole in the center, then score and pry it open slightly. Season the burrata with salt and pepper. Drizzle everything with the dressed peas and garnish with the herbs, pistachios, and a squeeze of lemon.

RED CHILI SEA BREAM CEVICHE

SERVES 2–4

Here's a great example of a dish that is always going to be better when prepared at home rather than in a restaurant. Because everything is made more or less to order, it's way trickier to do this in a busy professional kitchen. With this ceviche, I'm going for a mixture of textures and flavors: acid, of course, but also creaminess, a nice bright freshness from the herbs, punch from the onions and jalapeños, and texture from the radishes. Unlike some versions, the acid doesn't really cook the fish here. So it's definitely worth going to the trouble of buying the highest-quality, freshest sea bream you can for this recipe.

¼ cup thinly sliced red onions

½ tsp kosher salt

Juice of 2 limes

2 Tbsp Pasilla Chili Oil (page 227)

5–6 oz good-quality sea bream fillet (or another firm-fleshed white fish), skinned, pin bones removed, and diced

½ avocado, diced

½ cup diced Persian cucumbers

½ cup picked cilantro

1 green onion, sliced

2 radishes, thinly sliced

Tortilla chips, for serving

In a medium bowl, combine the red onions, salt, lime juice, and chili oil and let sit for 10 minutes. Add the fish, avocado, and cucumbers and toss everything to coat. Let marinate in the fridge for 10–20 minutes, then garnish with cilantro, green onions, and radishes. Serve immediately with tortilla chips.

RICOTTA & ZUCCHINI FRITTERS "CACIO E PEPE"

SERVES 6

We created this fritter/donut batter at the Harbord Room basically on day one, and its first use was for our Orange & Ricotta Dumplings (page 191), which quickly became one of our iconic desserts. The batter itself is super versatile, and here we're using it in a savory fritter preparation that yields a pillowy, melt-in-your-mouth interior and a crisp shell. These make a great canapé, and if you want to whip up a quick dipping sauce—although I don't think they need it—you could mix some mayonnaise with whatever hot sauce you have in the fridge and stir in a squeeze of fresh lemon juice.

1 large zucchini

1½ tsp kosher salt, divided

2 cups ricotta

Zest of 1 lemon

½ cup all-purpose flour

½ tsp baking powder

½ tsp sugar

½ tsp black pepper + extra for garnish

2 eggs + 1 yolk

Neutral oil, for frying

½ cup finely grated pecorino

In a medium bowl, grate the zucchini—you should wind up with about 2 cups. Add 1 tsp salt, toss to coat, and leave to sit for 30 minutes. Press the zucchini through a sieve to drain the liquid and set the zucchini aside.

With a stand mixer or in a bowl with a hand mixer or whisk, bring together the ricotta, lemon zest, flour, baking powder, sugar, remaining ½ tsp salt, pepper, and zucchini until smooth. With the mixer running, add the eggs and egg yolk one at a time, waiting until fully incorporated before adding the next.

In a heavy-bottomed pot, heat the frying oil to 350°F. Using two tablespoons, scoop the mixture into the hot oil. Fry the fritters until golden brown, about 2 minutes per side. You will need to do this in batches and make sure to let the oil come back up to temperature between batches.

Once fried, set the fritters aside on paper towel to drain before gently and generously tossing them in the grated pecorino and fresh pepper. Serve immediately either on their own or with some fresh lemon wedges and a spicy aioli on the side.

BAKED GNOCCHI WITH TOMATOES & MOZZARELLA

Gnocchi seems like this heroic endeavor, but the fact of the matter is, it's dead easy. The bulk of the work, such as it is, can also be done the day before so there's more time for canoodling on date night proper. It's one of those things you just have to make once to see how simple it is. The only tricks are to use a good, starchy potato (like russet or an old Yukon Gold), bake them, then slice them open right when they're still hot to let all that steam disappear. That way you're working with dry, starchy potatoes. After that, the ratios are 3, 2, 1: three parts potato, two parts flour, one egg, and then your seasoning—Parmigiano-Reggiano, salt, pepper, and lemon in this case. I like to work the dough on a dry surface to get that nice Play-Doh consistency, and then add flour. For this recipe, the objective is to have these things come out of the oven completely swollen into blissful, cushiony bites that are saturated with the tomato sauce.

SERVES 4 + LEFTOVERS

3 lb starchy potatoes (Yukon Gold or russet)

1 cup all-purpose flour + extra for rolling

1 egg + 1 yolk

¼ cup grated Parmigiano-Reggiano

1 tsp lemon zest

1 tsp kosher salt

¼ tsp black pepper

2 cups homemade tomato sauce or good-quality store-bought

½ cup packed basil leaves

5 oz Fior di Latte or fresh mozzarella, torn

2 Tbsp olive oil

Preheat the oven to 400°F. Using a fork, puncture each potato with a series of holes. This ensures the steam can escape. Bake the potatoes on a baking sheet until completely softened, about 45 minutes. Remove from the oven and immediately slice open. This allows the steam to escape and prevents any extra moisture developing. Once the potatoes are cool enough to handle, scoop out the insides and pass through a ricer or fine-mesh sieve.

In a bowl, combine the riced potatoes, flour, egg, egg yolk, Parmigiano-Reggiano, lemon zest, salt, and pepper. Using your hands, mix everything together just until a homogeneous dough forms and there aren't streaks of egg or flour running through, being careful not to overmix.

On a clean surface, roll the dough into an even log. Divide the log into six even pieces. Using both hands, roll out each piece to about ½ inch thick (about 1½ feet long). Flour each log generously, and, using a floured chef's knife or metal bench scraper, cut the log into ¾-inch pieces. Use the knife or bench scraper to move the gnocchi onto a floured baking sheet. Keep in the fridge until ready to use. If you want to save some for later, you can freeze a portion of the gnocchi on the baking sheet in a single layer and then transfer to a ziplock bag or airtight container for long-term storage, up to 1 month.

In a large pot of generously salted boiling water, cook the gnocchi in batches for 2–3 minutes, or just until they float. Remove the gnocchi to a large bowl with a slotted spoon or a spider.

Toss the cooked gnocchi in the tomato sauce and place in a large casserole dish. Top with basil and torn cheese. Bake at 425°F until golden brown and bubbly on top, about 15 minutes. Drizzle with olive oil and serve.

SWEET PEA & LEMON RISOTTO WITH ASPARAGUS

SERVES 4–6

People are sometimes intimidated by risotto—they think it's this finicky, hands-on dish that can't be left unattended for even 2 minutes. That's a misconception. Remember, you're just cooking rice. If you want to be precious about it, just be sure to get the initial cooking of the onions right: low and slow. After that, you can take your eyes off it; it's not a toddler. Even if the rice gets a little toasted, it always comes out. I like mine a little bit toothy and a little bit loose and luxurious. This recipe is almost more of a technique than a recipe. Once you've got this version under your belt, you can remix it in any number of ways. It's a what's-in-your-fridge type of situation.

1 bunch asparagus, woody stems removed

6 cups chicken or vegetable stock, divided

1½ cups blanched or frozen sweet peas, divided

Zest and juice of 1 lemon

½ cup basil leaves + 6 finely sliced leaves, for garnish

½ cup mint leaves + 6 finely sliced leaves, for garnish

Kosher salt

3 Tbsp olive oil + extra for garnish

1 medium onion, finely diced

2 cloves garlic, finely diced

2 cups arborio or carnaroli rice

1 cup dry white wine

1 bunch spinach

¼ cup butter

1 cup finely grated Parmigiano-Reggiano, divided

Black pepper

Cut the asparagus on a ½-inch bias, reserving the tips.

In a blender, combine ½ cup stock, ¾ cup asparagus pieces, ¾ cup peas, lemon zest and juice, basil, mint, and 1 tsp salt. Blend until smooth, and set aside.

In a medium pot, bring the remaining 5½ cups stock to a simmer. This will ensure that the stock is at the same temperature as the rice so as not to halt the cooking process.

In a heavy-bottomed pot over medium-low heat, heat the olive oil, onions, garlic, and a pinch of salt until the mixture is fully soft, about 20 minutes. Add the rice and gently toast for 5 minutes, until just barely golden. Add the white wine and cook until almost evaporated, about 2 minutes. Increase the heat to medium and add 2 cups stock to start. Continue to add in the stock in ½-cup increments to maintain the total amount of liquid, stirring occasionally. After 20 minutes of this process, the rice should be al dente. At this point, do not add any more stock.

Cook down until soupy, but not brothy, and the liquid is almost completely absorbed. Add in the blended asparagus mixture, the remaining asparagus and ¾ cup peas, and the spinach. Stir until the spinach has wilted completely, about 30 seconds. Stirring vigorously, add the butter and ¾ cup Parmigiano-Reggiano. Season with salt and pepper to taste. Serve immediately with the remaining ¼ cup Parmigiano-Reggiano and top with salt, pepper, basil, mint, and a drizzle of olive oil.

RISOTTO: The way I do risotto, especially when there's a vegetable component, is to make a puree with the main vegetable that's going in the dish. I do that to boost the flavor and the color. I quite like a creamy risotto, but what I don't like is a lot of butter, so I can cheat it a bit by adding a little less butter than usual and adding a little more puree. It boosts the body of the risotto and contributes to the underlying flavor. If it's wintertime and I'm doing a squash risotto, I'll do a bit of a squash puree. In the summer, I'll take some of the asparagus trimmings and some sweet peas and blend that up with a little stock, a bit of butter, and the herbs, and that gets fortified in the end with the last addition of butter. This is also a good way to use up those trimmings. The flavors are much more accentuated by adding them at the end rather than cooking with the risotto.

BAKED HALIBUT WITH SPRING VEGETABLES & SWEET PEA HUMMUS

SERVES 4

People are blown away by this recipe, but it couldn't be easier. You can even prep it ahead of time and have it ready so that on date night it only takes the time to throw the pan in the oven and serve it. The hummus is one of those things that's great to have in the fridge as a chip-and-dip component. It's healthier and lighter than a regular hummus and definitely has more of a summery, vibrant character. I'm more a fan of baked fish than seared fish because I like when the flesh is silky all the way through. Use any kind of white fish for this recipe and lots of aromatics, like lemon slices, dill, parsley, and green olives to mimic the Middle Eastern flavors you'd think of with hummus. The cherry tomatoes burst and their juices trickle down into the olive oil to form the backbone of the sauce, while the citrus bleeds out its juice and the peels char a bit, so you end up with this rustic yet impressive-looking dish. If you're cooking only for two people, feel free to halve the recipe, or scale it up if you want to entertain a crowd.

4 Tbsp olive oil, divided, + extra for garnish

Kosher salt

Four 5 oz pieces halibut

1 bunch asparagus, woody ends removed

1 leek, white and pale green parts only, washed and sliced into ¼-inch rounds

1 small bulb fennel, core removed and thinly sliced

2 cups halved cherry tomatoes

½ cup pitted Castelvetrano olives

Black pepper

¼ tsp chili flakes

½ tsp fennel seeds

1 cup picked dill leaves, divided

1 cup parsley leaves, divided

4 slices lemon

2 cups Sweet Pea Hummus (page 67)

Preheat the oven to 425°F.

Heat a large, nonstick pan over medium-high heat. Add 1 Tbsp olive oil to the pan, and lightly salt the halibut. Sear the fish, flesh side down, for about 1 minute, until golden brown. Transfer to a plate.

Line a large baking sheet with parchment paper. In a medium bowl, toss the asparagus, leeks, fennel, tomatoes, and olives with 2 Tbsp olive oil and a few pinches of salt and pepper. Spread the dressed vegetables evenly on the baking sheet in a single layer. Lay the fish overtop, skin side up, and sprinkle with chili flakes, fennel seeds, 1 Tbsp olive oil, half of the dill, and half of the parsley, along with a lemon slice over each.

Bake until the vegetables are blistered and the fish is just cooked through, about 15 minutes. If you are unsure, a good indicator is that the skin should peel off easily without any effort. The center of the fish should be glistening and juicy, with a slight translucent quality.

To serve, spread a generous amount of the sweet pea hummus on a serving platter, transfer all of the vegetables and their juices over the hummus, peel the skin off the fish, and lay the fish seared side up over the vegetables. Garnish with a drizzle of olive oil and the remaining fresh dill and parsley.

SEARED SCALLOPS WITH FRESH CORN POLENTA, FAVA BEANS, CHERRY TOMATOES & HERB OIL

This dish is a perfect date night meal. It's filling but not overly so, and just fancy enough. The bright green and deeply flavorful herb oil tastes fantastic, but also gives a real visual slap thanks to the way it sets off the bright yellow of the polenta. The polenta by itself is a star, and though it cooks for quite a while, the time is mostly hands-off, and it can be used in any number of recipes to highlight the flavor of peak season summer corn. Serve it anywhere you would creamed corn: as a side with baked ham, barbecued ribs, or fried chicken.

SERVES 4

1½ lb fava beans in the pod (1–1½ cups shelled beans)

12 heirloom cherry tomatoes

½ tsp kosher salt + extra for seasoning

½ small shallot, minced

1 clove garlic, crushed

12 large diver scallops

Black pepper

Neutral oil, for cooking

1 Tbsp butter

Fresh Corn Polenta (page 185), warmed

1 cup watercress, tender leaves picked

6 sprigs dill, for garnish

HERB OIL

½ cup olive oil

½ clove garlic

½ tsp kosher salt

¼ tsp pepper

½ cup packed basil leaves

½ cup packed mint leaves

½ cup packed parsley leaves

Juice of 1 lemon

2 ice cubes

Shell the fava beans from their pods. In a large saucepan, bring well-salted water to a boil over high heat. In a bowl, combine tap water and ice to make an ice bath, then set aside. Add the shelled beans to the boiling water and cook for about 3 minutes, then remove from the saucepan and immediately plunge them into the ice bath to halt the cooking. Let the beans cool, then peel the skins. Set aside. In the same saucepan, use a slotted spoon to slip the cherry tomatoes in for 10 seconds, then remove from the saucepan and immediately plunge them into the ice bath. Set aside.

Combine all the herb oil ingredients in a blender and blend on high until just smooth, taking care not to overheat.

Remove the skins of the cherry tomatoes, and place the peeled tomatoes in a small bowl with ½ tsp salt. Toss with the shallots and garlic, and allow this mixture to marinate for about 20 minutes. Add the fava beans and herb oil and stir to combine.

Pat the scallops dry with a paper towel, then season on both sides with salt and pepper. Heat a large cast-iron pan over medium-high heat. Coat the pan generously with neutral oil. When the oil begins to shimmer, add the scallops, taking care not to crowd the pan (depending on the size of your pan, this may need to be done in batches). Cook on the first side without moving for 2 minutes, until the edges develop a deep golden brown crust and the scallops release easily from the pan. Carefully flip the scallops and add the butter, basting the scallops for 45 seconds to 1 minute. Remove from the heat.

Spoon the polenta generously onto a serving platter, or onto individual serving dishes. Make a small well in the middle. Place watercress in the center and then the scallops overtop. Spoon the tomato and fava bean mixture overtop, garnish with the dill, and serve immediately.

FRESH CORN POLENTA

6 ears fresh corn, kernels cut off the cob (about 6 cups)

1½ tsp kosher salt

⅓ cup butter, diced

½ cup grated Parmigiano-Reggiano

1 Tbsp cold butter

Preheat the oven to 300°F.

In a blender, blend the fresh corn and salt on high speed for 2 minutes, or until completely smooth. Don't rush this step—you want it as smooth as possible. Pour the corn into a 10-inch baking dish. Evenly disperse the diced pieces of butter overtop, cover with aluminum foil, and bake for 2 hours, stirring every 30 minutes.

When the polenta has finished cooking in the oven, remove from the baking dish and transfer to a medium saucepot set over medium heat. Whisk in the Parmigiano-Reggiano and cold butter, and continue to whisk until everything is fully incorporated. Serve hot.

DOUBLE CHOCOLATE PEANUT BUTTER & SEA SALT COOKIES

MAKES 3 DOZEN COOKIES

¼ cup + 1 Tbsp smooth natural peanut butter

3 Tbsp butter

1¾ cups icing sugar

¾ cup cocoa powder

2 eggs

Pinch kosher salt

6 oz 70% semisweet chocolate, coarsely chopped

Chopped toasted peanuts

Flaky salt

So long as you don't suffer from a peanut allergy, you are going to love these cookies, and so will everyone you know. Chocolate and peanut butter, as the old commercials say, are two great tastes that go great together. You'll want natural peanut butter for these, not the admittedly delicious name-brand kind with all the maltodextrin and sugar, or else the cookies will be too sweet by half. If you're prepping for date night while you're still on dad duty, don't forget to let the kids lick the paddle of the stand mixer clean, and if they're careful, they can add the sprinkle of good-quality finishing salt and chopped peanuts at the end.

Preheat the oven to 350°F and line a baking sheet with parchment paper.

In the bowl of a stand mixer fitted with the paddle attachment, or in a large bowl with a hand mixer, cream the peanut butter and butter until smooth. Add the icing sugar and cocoa powder and mix on low speed until smooth. Add the eggs one at a time, mixing well before the second addition. Mix in the salt, then fold in the chopped chocolate. Transfer the dough to the fridge to rest for at least 30 minutes (or you can make this ahead and keep the dough for up to 3 days in the fridge or for up to 3 months in the freezer).

Using two spoons, scoop out a ball of dough about 1½ Tbsp in size. Roll the ball gently in your hands, then flatten out slightly on the parchment paper using the back of a spoon or the palm of your hand. Repeat with the remaining dough. Sprinkle the tops with chopped peanuts and a pinch of flaky salt.

Bake for 10–12 minutes, or until the tops just begin to crack. Remove from the oven and allow to cool completely.

SOFT-SET DARK CHOCOLATE TART

This is one of those recipes where you want to use the best possible chocolate you can get hold of. Spend whatever amount of money you're comfortable with—a less expensive chocolate tart is still going to be incredible, but if you've got access to something special, here's where to use it. The flavor comes out so intensely, it's like the purest form of chocolate in a dessert that I've ever had. The recipe itself is super simple and the pastry can be used in lots of different places—just keep it in the freezer and pull it out whenever you need it. The only trick is that it needs to be baked and consumed within a couple of hours so that it retains its silky, luxurious mouthfeel. Happily, once you blind-bake the crust and have the filling done, you can let them sit (separately); just before sitting down to eat, you can pour the filling into the crust, put it in the oven, and let it bake for 20 minutes and then sit for 20 minutes. When you serve it, it will be absolutely peaking.

MAKES ONE 9-INCH TART

PASTRY

1⅓ cups all-purpose flour

¾ cup icing sugar

7 Tbsp very cold butter, cut into small cubes

Pinch kosher salt

2 egg yolks

CHOCOLATE FILLING

10½ oz good-quality 70% dark chocolate (see sidebar, page 190)

1¼ cups heavy cream

¼ cup half & half cream

2 eggs, whisked

In a food processor, pulse the flour, icing sugar, butter, and salt until the butter incorporates into the flour. Take care not to overmix; the texture should resemble oats. If you don't have a food processor, use a pastry cutter and medium bowl.

Add the egg yolks and continue pulsing until it just begins to form a smooth consistency. If you don't have a food processor, use an electric mixer until the dough forms together. Remove the dough and, with your hands, quickly work into a uniform ball, bringing any loose flour into the ball. Place the dough between two sheets of parchment paper and roll out to a 6-inch disk, about 1 inch thick. Let the dough rest in the fridge for at least 1 hour.

Keep the parchment paper edges loose to allow the dough to be rolled out easily. Rolling the dough out between parchment helps keep your hands from warming the dough and allows you to get it as thin as possible. Also, there is no need to flour the surface, and it makes for easier handling when transferring to the tart shell.

Roll the pastry out to an 11- or 12-inch square, just large enough to line a 9-inch tart shell with a slight overhang. Press the dough into the corners with your fingers. If there are any cracks, you can patch them up with extra dough trimmings. Pierce the dough all over with a fork. Return to the fridge for 1 hour before baking.

→ Continued . . .

After about 50 minutes of resting the dough, preheat the oven to 350°F for 10 minutes. Bake the shell for 20–25 minutes, until it's evenly golden brown.

Chop the chocolate into very small pieces and place in a medium heatproof bowl. In a small saucepan, heat the heavy cream and half & half cream until hot, but don't boil. Pour the cream mixture over the chocolate and stir until melted. Whisk in the eggs until incorporated.

Cool the oven to 300°F. Pour the mixture into the baked tart shell, taking care not to spill any on the edges. Bake in the center of the oven for 18–20 minutes. The chocolate should be set for all but the middle 2 inches, which should still jiggle when lightly tapped. The surface should have a glossy, mirror-like finish with no cracks and a silky-smooth, soft texture when cut. Cool the tart slightly, remove from the pan, and serve with lightly whipped cream and fresh berries.

KITCHEN TIP: This recipe is a take on a short crust—it's very quick to prepare and easy to work with. It's measured out to fit a 9-inch pan ¾ inch deep. If you like, you can make small, individual tarts using a muffin tin.

CHOCOLATE: My introduction to what proper chocolate should taste and feel like came during my first year at the Stratford Chefs School. The incredible pastry chef, John Bex, made it his personal mission to turn us all into chocolate snobs. I remember he laid out a selection of great chocolates from around the world and we did a tasting. It was like a light went on and I suddenly realized what great chocolate meant. Good chocolate should be tasted with a wine-like mindset: How's the mouthfeel? What do you smell? What flavors reveal themselves over time as you roll it around your palate? Having said that, I think I still eat my weight in peanut M&Ms every year.

ORANGE & RICOTTA DUMPLINGS

SERVES 6–8

We used to serve these all the time at the Harbord Room, but the challenge at the restaurant was getting the timing right. You can't really hold them, and they have to be cooked fresh to order. That's difficult in a small, busy restaurant, but that's exactly why they're perfect for a home cook. These are great for a date night, but also when entertaining a few friends. They've got about a 2-minute window when they're absolutely perfect, so at home I'll cook up a few at a time and then put them right on the table and let people fight it out among themselves until the next batch is ready. There's no better sweet bite as far as I'm concerned.

1 cup + 2½ Tbsp sugar, divided

1 Tbsp cinnamon

2 cups ricotta

½ cup all-purpose flour

½ tsp baking powder

Pinch kosher salt

Zest of 2 oranges

2 eggs + 1 yolk

Neutral oil, for frying

½ batch Lemon Curd (page 222), for serving

In a medium bowl, mix 1 cup sugar with the cinnamon and set aside.

With a stand mixer or in a bowl with a hand mixer or whisk, bring together the ricotta, flour, baking powder, remaining 2½ Tbsp sugar, salt, and orange zest until very smooth. With the mixer running, add the eggs and egg yolk, one at a time, waiting until fully incorporated before adding the next.

In a heavy-bottomed pot, heat the frying oil to 350°F. Using a tablespoon, scoop the batter into the hot oil. Fry until golden brown, about 2 minutes per side. You'll need to do this in batches and allow the oil to come back up to temperature between batches. Once cooked, transfer the dumplings to a plate lined with paper towel to drain, then gently toss in the cinnamon sugar mixture. Serve immediately with lemon curd.

KITCHEN TIP: Deep-frying at home is definitely a treat, but you don't need to be intimidated by it. Deep-frying is actually a dry-heat cooking method, and if you're frying at the right temperature, the food doesn't take on much oil at all. For that reason, it's worth investing in a standard fryer thermometer—they're widely available and relatively cheap. The oil itself can be filtered and saved for the next time, so it's not wasteful. I put mine through a coffee filter and then just put it back in a bottle and store it in the fridge or the cupboard.

PITMASTER
(KEEP TELLING YOURSELF THAT)

"TO BARBECUE IS A WAY OF LIFE RATHER THAN A DESIRABLE METHOD OF COOKING."

—CLEMENT FREUD

From time immemorial, the natural cooking habitat of dads the world over was, is, and always will be the grill. Even if an old-school dad never so much as set foot in the kitchen, couldn't tell a cucumber from a cantaloupe, and thought that Jacques Pépin was an amorous cartoon skunk, the barbecue was his domain. Stubby in hand, novelty apron untied for maximum comfort, he was a tong-wielding, flame-adjusting king surveying his yard and all those who roughhoused within its fence-post borders.

Inevitably, the results of these fair-weather grillers lacked something in the way of culinary finesse: steaks indistinguishable from the briquettes they were burned over, blackened chicken sashimi, desiccated patties, weather-beaten wieners. What they lacked in flavor they made up for in conviction, however, because there's something about cooking outside, over fire, that dads find irresistible.

A NOTE ABOUT COOKING METHODS: Cory developed the recipes in this chapter over charcoal, and that's the method he prefers, but he's not maniacal about it. There is something romantic about putting in the time to learn about coals, how they work, and the flavor they add, but ultimately, it's up to you whether to use charcoal, gas, hardwood, or whatever you're comfortable with. The results will be more or less equal.

In this chapter, we're aiming to take the modern dad beyond just the standard patties and wieners repertoire and explore a more nuanced survey of what the barbecue is capable of. Cory's approach to the grill covers everything from salads to whole fish. The goal is to turn out well-rounded pitmasters, as comfortable with a bunch of asparagus and a whole sea bream as they are with short ribs and grilled chicken. There will, of course, be steak too.

Of all the ways of getting food on the table, cooking outdoors is easily the most social. Typically, you're moving the whole cooking experience and setup outside to where your guests are, so you're hosting while you're cooking and the cooking itself becomes part of the entertainment.

While most people think of grilling as a summertime activity, and it certainly is the most grill-friendly season, there's plenty to be said for firing up the coals, or lighting the burners, all year round. A decent headlamp and a warm pair of gloves will extend your grilling season to cover even the darkest days of winter. In the same way that firing up the grill saves you from turning on the stove and heating up the house in the dog days of summer, that scenario is flipped in the winter and the grill provides a warm cooking place to gather around.

GRILLED CAESAR SALAD

SERVES 4

4 slices thick-cut sourdough bread, torn into 1-inch pieces

Olive oil

Kosher salt and black pepper

¾ cup grated Parmigiano-Reggiano, divided

3 hearts romaine, halved

¾ cup Caesar Salad Dressing (page 226)

3 pieces crispy bacon, crumbled

Lemon wedge, for serving

I was strongly opposed to grilled lettuce when it started to become a thing a decade or so ago. It just seemed like overkill and another overhyped food trend that would quickly disappear. Eventually I relented and gave it a try, and I had to admit that I was wrong. Grilled romaine is a treat. The smoky, almost caramelized quality that the grill lends to the lettuce complements and brings out all the richness of the dressing. It might no longer be trendy, but I still make it all the time.

Preheat the oven to 375°F and line a baking sheet with parchment paper.

In a mixing bowl, toss the sourdough bread pieces with 2 Tbsp olive oil, a pinch of salt, and a grind of pepper. Arrange in a single layer on the baking sheet and sprinkle evenly with ¼ cup Parmigiano-Reggiano. Bake for 12–15 minutes, until crispy and golden brown on the edges. Set aside.

Dress each romaine heart with olive oil, salt, and pepper, ensuring that every nook and cranny has been seasoned. On a barbecue over medium-high heat, place the romaine, cut side down, on the grill and cook until slightly wilted and charred, about 3 minutes. Remove from the heat and arrange on a platter. Drizzle with Caesar dressing, then garnish with the croutons, bacon bits, and remaining ½ cup grated Parmigiano-Reggiano. Serve with a lemon wedge on the side.

GRILLED VEGETABLES WITH CHIMICHURRI

SERVES 8

Here's a great opportunity to really vibe with your barbecue. I love the idea of taking a bunch of fresh summer ingredients—whole baby turnips, radishes, peppers, corn, zucchini, pattypan squash, eggplant—and just throwing everything on the grill, skin on, and letting it ride. Don't be afraid of the smoke. Don't be afraid of char marks. Don't be afraid of what you think is burning something, because these ingredients, with their protective outer skins, want to be cooked until you think they're burned. Chimichurri is a great sauce to have in your repertoire, and although it's most famously served with steak, it goes beautifully with the smokiness and brings out the meatiness of these vegetables.

1 sweet potato, sliced in ⅓-inch rounds

1 red onion, peeled and sliced into ½-inch rounds

4 tender white turnips, tops trimmed and halved

2 handfuls oyster mushrooms, torn into small clusters

1 yellow zucchini, quartered lengthwise, spongy core removed

1 green zucchini, quartered lengthwise, spongy core removed

1 bunch broccolini

1 bunch asparagus, woody ends removed

1 handful garlic scapes (if you can find them), woody bases trimmed about 2 inches from bottom

Olive oil

Kosher salt

Black pepper

Splash of red wine vinegar

1 cup Chimichurri (page 227)

Grilled vegetables are all about the preparation and staggering the cooking according to which vegetables take the longest. Lightly oil and season your vegetables with salt and pepper, keeping them in separate piles on a baking sheet.

Start with a hot, clean, and oiled grill: lay the sweet potato and red onion slices down first, as these are the densest and will need a head start. Working in batches, grill and char the vegetables on all sides—as a loose rule, sweet potatoes and onions will take 10–12 minutes; tender turnips and mushrooms will take 6–8 minutes; and zucchini, broccolini, asparagus, and garlic scapes will take 4–5 minutes.

The key to nice grill marks is to not shift the vegetables around too much on the grill—let them sit in one spot and char, as too much handling lowers the surface heat on the grill, and that's when you get steaming and sticking.

Arrange your grilled vegetables on a big platter, give them a splash of red wine vinegar and a drizzle of chimichurri, and serve with a small bowl of additional chimichurri in the center for dipping.

FLOCK SPICED GRILLED SPATCHCOCKED CHICKEN

SERVES 4

This is the spice blend we use on our rotisserie chickens at all the Flock restaurants. We spent a long time figuring out the right sugar-salt-spice ratio to allow for the optimal level of browning. At the restaurant, we cook these birds on a spit, but at home there's no better method than spatchcocking, where you remove the backbone and lay the bird out flat. It's virtually foolproof. I start the bird on the skin side for 5 minutes, then flip it onto the bone side for the remainder because it acts as a natural kind of insulation to prevent the bird from overcooking. As long as you start the ball rolling with a crisp skin and then finish it with the lid on so you get that nicely conducted heat, you're going to end up with that super-golden, crispy, puffed-up skin that's so appealing.

One 3 lb whole chicken

2–3 Tbsp Flock Chicken Dry Rub (page 228)

Cooking oil

Pat the chicken dry with paper towel and set it on a cutting board. Flip it onto its breast and, using sturdy kitchen shears, remove the backbone by cutting carefully down each side of the bone with ½ inch to spare on either side of the spine, starting at the head end of the bird and going all the way down to the butt. The entire inside of the chicken should be exposed when you're finished. Once the backbone is out, flip the chicken back over and press down on the breastbone to crack it and flatten the chicken out further.

Generously coat both sides of the chicken with the dry rub, ensuring that it gets in all the nooks and crannies of the skin. Place on a rack, uncovered, in the fridge and allow it to air-cure for at least 4 hours and up to 1 day.

On a barbecue over medium-high heat, lightly grease the grill with the neutral oil. Lightly oil the chicken on both sides before placing on the grill, skin side down and on a 45-degree angle to the grates. Cook for 5 minutes, or until the skin releases easily from the grill—don't move it during this time. Pivot the bird 45 degrees, still skin side down (this will give the desired crosshatched grill marks), and cook for another 5 minutes. Flip the chicken and cook, bone side down, for 30 minutes or until the fattest part of the meat reaches an internal temperature of 165°F and the juices run clear. Allow to rest for 15 minutes before serving.

PRAWN & TUNA BURGERS

This is the pescatarian answer to the Smashburger. I created this recipe because I wanted a fish burger that still had the bite of a hamburger. Usually, I don't like too much done with my fish. I don't like mousses, I'm not big into purees, and for a fish burger I didn't want salmon mixed with mayonnaise mixed with this and that, so I came up with this version using prawns. I blend half of the prawns with the flavoring and mix that with the chopped prawns, and with the salt in there, a bit of soy sauce, and the acid, it almost gels together so you can cook it like a regular burger. It's got tons of flavor from ginger, green onions, and jalapeños. Then it's just a matter of piling on the textures: thick-cut, charred sweet-and-sour red onions that have been given a very quick pickle with red wine vinegar, cilantro, more jalapeños, and a bit of sesame oil, and then you toss the shiitake mushrooms in there as well. It's a real summer hit.

SERVES 6

8 oz ahi or albacore tuna, diced small

8 oz prawns, minced

2 Tbsp chopped cilantro

1 green onion, sliced

1 Tbsp minced jalapeños

2 tsp kosher salt

½ tsp pepper

1 Tbsp grated ginger

1 clove garlic, grated

2 Tbsp soy sauce

1 Tbsp sesame oil

1 egg white

2 Tbsp neutral oil (optional)

6 burger buns

TOPPINGS

Sweet & Sour Charred Red Onions & Shiitake Mushrooms (page 213)

Lettuce leaves

Avocado

Cilantro

Dijon mustard

Mayonnaise

¼ cup cilantro sprigs

In a medium bowl, combine the tuna, prawns, cilantro, green onions, jalapeños, salt, pepper, ginger, garlic, soy sauce, sesame oil, and egg white and mix vigorously until the mixture has almost emulsified. Using your hands or a ring mold, form six equal patties. Place on a baking sheet lined with parchment paper and refrigerate for 1–3 hours to allow the patties to solidify.

On a really hot, clean barbecue or in a cast-iron pan with 2 Tbsp neutral cooking oil, cook the burgers for 3 minutes per side. Pay extra attention when flipping the burgers, as they can be quite delicate.

Serve immediately on soft, toasted buns topped with the red onions and shiitake mushrooms, lettuce, avocado, cilantro, and a mixture of Dijon mustard and mayo.

KITCHEN TIP: The grilled pickled onions and mushrooms in this recipe are extremely versatile, and it's worth making an extra batch to keep in the fridge (if you can avoid eating them all in one go). They've got a little acid and a little sweetness and lots of aromatics, so they're a great accompaniment to any kind of fish dish, on a sandwich, alongside some chops, or as part of a steak plate with crispy potatoes.

GRILLED WHOLE FISH WITH ROMESCO SAUCE

SERVES 2

1½–2 lb whole dressed firm-fleshed white fish (such as sea bream, branzino, or snapper; ask your fishmonger to dress it)

Olive oil

Kosher salt

Black pepper

3 sprigs parsley

3 slices lemon

GARNISH

1 lemon, halved

½ cup Romesco Sauce (page 226)

Drizzle of olive oil

Flaky salt

If you want to take the fear factor out of grilling a whole fish, it's worth investing in a fish basket. It will also come in handy when grilling vegetables, so the small investment will soon pay for itself. Strictly speaking, though, as long as your grill is clean and hot, you don't really need one. Romesco is an absolute killer sauce to know how to make and has a million uses, including in a couple of other places in this book, and the combination with the smoky, grilled fish is a sure fire winner.

The real secret to a perfectly grilled fish is the heat of the grill and the preparation of the fish. To score the fish, take a sharp knife and, using just the tip, make small cuts down either side of the spine and just underneath the dorsal fin, down the belly, and around the gills. Essentially, we are outlining the fillet that we'll remove after grilling. Don't go too deep with the scoring. For the spine, stop when you hit bone; in the case of the belly, a shallow cut that juts through the skin without cutting all the way through is ideal. Stay as close to the spine, tail, gills, and belly as you can so that as much of the flesh stays on the fillet as possible. The goal here is a fillet that, after grilling, lifts perfectly off the bone with just a spoon and fork, with no meticulous serving work.

Wipe the skin and cavity of the fish with paper towel, taking off as much of the surface moisture as you can. Rub generously with olive oil, salt, and pepper and place the parsley and lemon slices in the cavity.

Place the seasoned fish on a clean, very hot grill at a 45-degree angle to the grill grates. Once the fish is on the grill, you won't be moving it around—we're not trying to achieve a crisscross pattern or any other nonsense. Fish skin is very temperamental and needs to cook long enough so that it crisps and releases from the grill, or you'll be left with messy pieces of skin attached to the grill, not the fish.

Place the lemon halves on the grill, flesh side down, and leave alone to char.

Leave the fish to cook, without moving, for 5 minutes, then attempt to lift it up just slightly. If the skin comes away from the grill easily and is slightly charred and crispy, then it's perfect. Roll the fish over and cook in the same manner on the second side. You can check for doneness by taking a paring knife and looking at the fattest part of the fish at the bone—if it's the slightest bit translucent and flaky, it's done.

Remove the fish and the lemon halves from the grill, place them on a platter, and serve with romesco sauce, a drizzle of olive oil, and flaky salt.

BARBECUE POMEGRANATE SHORT RIBS

Here we're using those classic, English-cut, Fred Flintstone–looking short ribs. The big ones. One rib per person kind of thing. They get dressed in this rich marinade—don't worry about giving them the full 24-hour treatment; if you can, great, but it's not make-or-break—and then wrapped up in aluminum foil with a couple of ice cubes. The ice cubes melt, obviously, and help create a kind of braising process in the packets, binding together with the juice and drippings that come out of the ribs. It's crazy. Anyway, these are pretty hands-off ribs. Once they're on the grill you can basically just leave them, so long as the temperature remains fairly consistent. After a few hours, you carefully take them out of the foil, reserving all that sauce they've created, throw the ribs over some high heat, and give them a heavy baste every few minutes. By the time you've used up all that sauce, you'll have these crusty, tender, but not exactly falling-off-the-bone ribs your children's children will tell their children about.

SERVES 4

⅓ cup packed brown sugar

⅓ cup pomegranate molasses

1 tsp smoked paprika

1 clove garlic, grated

1 Tbsp apple cider vinegar

⅔ cup ketchup

1 Tbsp Dijon mustard

1 Tbsp Worcestershire sauce

1 tsp kosher salt

1 tsp black pepper

4 portions (about 1½ lb each) bone-in short ribs

4 ice cubes

Handful pomegranate seeds

1 green onion, thinly sliced

Handful toasted sesame seeds

1 long red chili, sliced, for garnish

6 sprigs cilantro, for garnish

Sweet & Sour Charred Red Onions & Shiitake Mushrooms (page 213; optional)

In a large bowl, combine the brown sugar, pomegranate molasses, paprika, garlic, apple cider vinegar, ketchup, Dijon, Worcestershire, salt, and pepper. Add the short ribs and massage to coat before marinating in the fridge for 2 hours or up to overnight.

Preheat the grill to low, or about 300°F, creating a section where the heat is indirect (or without flames). Using a double layer of heavy-duty aluminum foil, create two packages and fill with the short ribs, all of the marinade, and 2 ice cubes in each, wrapping the meat well and ensuring that steam and liquid cannot escape. Make sure all the edges are very well sealed.

Cook over indirect heat for 2½ hours, turning over halfway through without opening the packages. After 2½ hours, carefully open one package to check for doneness—the meat should be fork-tender, but not falling off the bone. If it's not yet fork-tender, close the package back up and continue to cook, checking every 15 minutes. (You do not want to overcook to the point where the meat is pulling away from the bone.) Reserving the excess marinade, remove the meat from the foil and grill it over a very low flame, basting with the remaining marinade and turning frequently, until you have developed a sticky glazed and charred exterior. This should take about 30 minutes. Garnish the ribs with pomegranate seeds, green onions, sesame seeds, red chili, cilantro, and sweet & sour charred red onions and shiitake mushrooms.

GRILLED STEAK

SERVES 2

One 1½ lb bone-in rib steak, about 1½ inches thick

Kosher salt and black pepper

2 cloves garlic, crushed

1 large sprig rosemary

2 sprigs thyme

2 Tbsp butter, cubed

2 sprigs parsley

Crusty on the outside and pink in the middle, the classic dad steak needs no introduction. This is as simple as it gets, but if you want to play around with adding a little compound butter action (smoked paprika and chives, or hot honey, Gorgonzola and rosemary), fill your boots.

Preheat the grill over high heat and oil lightly.

Season both sides of the steak generously with salt and pepper. Place the steak on the hot grill and cook without moving for about 3 minutes. Rotate the steak one-quarter turn (not flipping) and continue to cook for about 2 minutes, until well charred on the first side.

Flip the steak over and rub the charred side with the crushed garlic cloves, leaving them to sit on top. Pile the rosemary and thyme over the steak, and place the cubed butter overtop to drip down and absorb into the meat. It'll melt and the grill might flame up a bit, but that's what you're looking for. Let the steak cook this way for about 5 minutes, or to the desired doneness. For a steak this size, depending on the heat of your grill, 5 minutes will bring you to medium-rare, but adjust as you like.

Rest the steak for 7–10 minutes on a wire rack before serving with Crispy Smashed Pot-Roasted Potatoes (page 212). Garnish with parsley.

KITCHEN TIP: One of the most important parts of this recipe is resting the steak before serving or slicing. Place it on a wire rack so air can circulate. If you place it on a plate, you'll create a hot spot, which will cause the juices to pool around the meat.

CRISPY SMASHED POT-ROASTED POTATOES

SERVES 4–6

Everything great about potatoes in one recipe. You've got the crispiness of French fries, the deep, comforting goodness of roasted potatoes, and the creamy lusciousness of mashed. Excellent enough on their own, these potatoes really come alive thanks to the deep, mellow flavor of roasted shallots and garlic and the brightness from the thyme and rosemary. Smashing the boiled potatoes is fun, but if you're feeling generous, you can let the kids do it.

1½ lb mini potatoes

1 Tbsp olive oil

1 tsp kosher salt

½ tsp pepper

2 shallots, peeled and quartered

3 cloves garlic, smashed

6 sprigs thyme

2 sprigs rosemary

2 Tbsp butter

Preheat your grill over high heat or the oven to 400°F. Bring a large pot of well-salted water to a boil.

Boil the potatoes for 7–10 minutes, until tender, then set aside to drain well.

Once cool enough to handle, lightly crush the potatoes with a small saucepan until they break open. In a bowl, toss the potatoes with the olive oil, salt, and pepper. Arrange in a tightly packed single layer in a 10-inch cast-iron or heavy-bottomed pan, ensuring that all the potatoes are making contact with the bottom of the pan. Arrange the shallots, garlic, thyme, and rosemary over the potatoes. Fleck with little bits of butter.

If you're cooking this on the grill, place the entire cast-iron pan over direct heat. Cook the potatoes, without moving, until they just start to brown on the bottom, about 10 minutes. Flip them over and cook for an additional 10 minutes, until the potatoes, shallots, and garlic are tender and browned and the herbs are frizzled and fragrant.

If you're doing this in the oven, start the potatoes on the stove over medium heat. Cook the potatoes, without moving them, until just starting to brown on the bottom, about 5 minutes. Then transfer to the oven and bake for 30 minutes, until brown and crispy.

Serve inverted or as-is.

SWEET & SOUR CHARRED RED ONIONS & SHIITAKE MUSHROOMS

SERVES 4–6

If you're looking for a place to start in this book, this could be it. Charred onions, all floppy and smoky, are phenomenal things on their own, but accompany them with meaty, seared shiitake mushrooms and you've got an almost-spicy, sweet-and-sour, chunky condiment that you might be tempted to make into a meal on its own. They're great with a steak but wouldn't be out of place on some roasted pork, in a sandwich, or overtop some creamy polenta. I'm sure you won't have a problem finding somewhere to use them.

Zest and juice of 1 lime

1 Tbsp red wine vinegar

1 Tbsp thinly sliced jalapeños (¼ jalapeño)

1 Tbsp honey

1 tsp kosher salt

1 tsp sesame oil

2 Tbsp chopped cilantro

1 Tbsp soy sauce

2 red onions, peeled and cut into ½-inch slices

6 shiitake mushrooms, stems removed

2 Tbsp vegetable oil

Preheat your grill to high heat and oil lightly.

In a medium bowl, combine the lime zest and juice, red wine vinegar, jalapeños, honey, salt, sesame oil, cilantro, and soy sauce. Set aside.

In a separate bowl, toss the onions and shiitakes in the vegetable oil to coat, then place on the grill for about 3 minutes per side, until charred but still firm in the center—you'll finish cooking them in the dressing.

Immediately transfer to the bowl with the dressing and toss to coat. It's important to do this while the vegetables are still hot so they absorb the flavors. Cover and let steam for 15 minutes, then transfer to an airtight container and keep refrigerated until ready to use—I use this as a cold garnish on burgers, fish, grilled meats, and more.

GRILLED ASPARAGUS WITH ROMESCO

SERVES 2–4

Sometimes it's nice to carefully peel the bottom third of each individual asparagus spear and delicately steam them to a tender, elegant completion. Other times it's just about snapping off the fibrous ends and laying the tender stalks over some smoking-hot coals until they get some serious char. That's what these are. All that smoky grill flavor in the asparagus is there mainly to highlight the accompanying romesco sauce. The romesco is slightly more labor-intensive, which is why it makes sense to make a large batch. Besides, you can use romesco all over the place: with grilled leeks, with a nice piece of fish, or alongside some grilled steak.

1 bunch asparagus, woody ends removed

⅓ cup olive oil + extra for garnish

Kosher salt and black pepper

Romesco Sauce (page 226)

2 Tbsp Toasted Sourdough Breadcrumbs with Rosemary & Sea Salt (page 228; optional)

Preheat your grill to high heat, and oil lightly.

In a bowl, toss the asparagus in olive oil to coat, and season with salt and pepper. Place them on the grill perpendicular to the direction of the grates so that they don't fall through. Cook, without moving, for about 2 minutes, until blistered and charred. Roll the asparagus over (try to do this quickly, and multiple spears at once) and cook on the second side for another 2 minutes. You're looking for deep charring and a slightly firm center when you bite into the asparagus.

While the asparagus cooks, spread the base of a platter with the romesco sauce. Transfer the grilled asparagus to the platter overtop the sauce, and garnish with an extra drizzle of olive oil and the toasted sourdough breadcrumbs.

FUNDAMENTALS

"PROMISES AND PIE CRUST ARE MADE TO BE BROKEN."

—JONATHAN SWIFT

Hey, dad. Welcome to the final section of the book. Even though we're all the way at the back, don't sleep on these recipes. They're here not only because many of them show up as crucial elements of several recipes throughout these pages, but also because they are the kinds of recipes that, if you learn them, will help establish a solid foundation for all kinds of cooking. Dialing these in, and the techniques involved in bringing them to life, will give you a lot of confidence in the kitchen, whether you're cooking from this book, improvising something up at a vacation house, or coming up with dinner on a night when you clean out the fridge.

FLAKY PASTRY

MAKES 2 LARGE PIES, WITHOUT TOPS

2½ cups all-purpose flour

Pinch kosher salt

1 cup (½ lb) very cold butter

¾–1 cup ice water, or more as needed

This is a general all-purpose pastry that has a million applications. I've been using it for ages. The key to success with any pastry is not overhandling or overworking the dough. Especially with butter pastries, keep your hands off as much as possible to avoid warming the butter. Keep it cold and rest the dough for a good hour in between all mixing/rolling stages. This will relax the glutens (the protein in the flour) so the pastry doesn't shrink during baking.

In a medium bowl, whisk or sift the flour and salt until no lumps remain. Cut the butter into ¼-inch cubes and toss to coat in the flour. Place in the freezer to chill for at least 20 minutes.

When the butter-flour mixture is sufficiently chilled, press the butter into the flour until it is the size of walnut halves. Fill a cup measurement completely with ice and cover with water to fill. Allow to sit until the outside of the cup is ice-cold to the touch. Add ¾ cup water to the flour mixture a few tablespoons at a time and mix just until the dough comes together, adding more if needed. You should stop adding water as soon are you are able to see streaks of flour running through the dough.

Wrap the dough in plastic and allow it to rest, hydrate, and chill in the fridge before rolling, forming, and baking.

KITCHEN TIP: To save time, keep sticks of butter in the freezer and, using the largest hole in a box grater, grate the frozen butter into the flour to coat. This creates perfectly flat and distinct butter pieces.

LEMON CURD

MAKES ABOUT 1½ CUPS

1 cup sugar

Zest and juice of 3 lemons, divided

4 eggs

⅓ cup butter, chilled and cubed

In a bowl, combine the sugar and lemon zest. Rub the zest into the sugar vigorously with your fingers until it's clumpy and fragrant. This will release the lemon oil and make your lemon curd more fragrant.

Bring a saucepan filled with about 2 inches of water to a simmer over medium-high heat. Place a heatproof bowl overtop, making sure that the bottom of the bowl doesn't touch the water. Place the eggs, sugar mixture, and lemon juice in the bowl and whisk together. Cook the mixture over medium heat, stirring constantly, until it's thick and coats the back of a spoon. Remove the bowl and set aside to cool for about 5 minutes. Add the warm curd to a blender. Pulse until smooth, then add the cubes of butter one at a time, blending on high speed until emulsified. Cover the surface of the curd directly with plastic wrap and chill in the fridge to set for at least 3 hours. It'll last in the fridge for about 1 week.

ROASTED BEET & CITRUS DRESSING

MAKES ABOUT 2½ CUPS

1 small or medium red beet, halved (see tip)

1 small yellow onion, peeled and halved (see tip)

2 cloves garlic

½ cup packed basil leaves

¼ cup freshly squeezed orange juice

¼ cup freshly squeezed lemon juice

1 Tbsp Dijon mustard

1 Tbsp honey

½ Tbsp kosher salt

¼ tsp black pepper

¾ cup light-flavored olive oil or avocado oil

In a small pot, steam or boil the beet, onion, and garlic until fork-tender, 20–30 minutes.

Drain the vegetables and pat dry with a paper towel. Peel the beet, then place the onion, garlic, and beet in a blender along with the basil, orange juice, lemon juice, mustard, honey, salt, and pepper. Blend on high until smooth. Turn your blender down to medium and slowly pour in the oil to form a light emulsification.

Transfer to an airtight container and store in the fridge for up to 2 weeks.

KITCHEN TIP: The beet and onion should be on the smaller size—say slightly smaller than a tennis ball.

MISO, MAPLE & CITRUS DRESSING

MAKES ABOUT 3 CUPS

1 cup neutral oil

¼ cup maple syrup

¼ cup rice wine vinegar

¼ cup soy sauce

5 Tbsp water

5 Tbsp freshly squeezed
lemon juice

5 Tbsp white miso

2 Tbsp sesame oil

4 tsp grated ginger

1 tsp kosher salt

1 clove garlic

Combine all ingredients and blend until smooth. Store in a large jar or container and refrigerate until needed. You can halve this recipe if you like, or make the whole thing and use over the course of 2 weeks.

APPLE, THYME & SHALLOT VINAIGRETTE

MAKES ABOUT 1½ CUPS

2 shallots, finely diced

5 Tbsp white wine vinegar

2 tsp kosher salt

½ tsp black pepper

1 cup extra-virgin olive oil

½ cup finely chopped green apple

2 Tbsp maple syrup

2 Tbsp grainy mustard

2 tsp finely chopped thyme

In a mason jar, combine the shallots, white wine vinegar, salt, and pepper, and let sit for 20 minutes. After 20 minutes, add the olive oil, apple, maple syrup, grainy mustard, and thyme. Shake well and keep refrigerated for up to 1 week.

CRISPY PANCETTA & SHALLOT VINAIGRETTE

MAKES ABOUT 1 CUP

½ cup neutral oil

2 large shallots, finely diced

½ cup small-diced pancetta

3 Tbsp sherry vinegar

2 tsp grainy mustard

1 tsp finely chopped thyme

Black pepper

In a small saucepan over medium heat, combine the oil, shallots, and pancetta. Cook slowly until the pancetta has rendered its fat and is crispy and the shallots are caramelized. As soon as the pancetta and shallots are golden brown and crispy, add the vinegar directly into the pot to stop the cooking. Remove from heat and allow to cool. Add the mustard, thyme, and pepper. This is best served warm, but if you're keeping it in the fridge, you'll need to warm it back up before serving. It will keep for 1 week.

BUTTERMILK AVOCADO RANCH

MAKES ABOUT 2¼ CUPS

¾ cup buttermilk

½ cup dill

½ cup diced Persian cucumbers

¼ cup full-fat mayonnaise

1 tsp black pepper

¾ tsp kosher salt

½ jalapeño, seeded

½ clove garlic

½ large ripe avocado

Juice of 1 lemon

Combine all ingredients in a blender or food processor and pulse until smooth. Keep refrigerated.

GREEN TAHINI DRESSING

MAKES ABOUT 2 CUPS

1 cup picked basil leaves

1 cup picked parsley leaves

1 cup picked cilantro leaves

1 cup picked mint leaves

1½ cloves garlic

1 jalapeño, halved and seeded

⅓ cup rice wine vinegar

3 Tbsp olive oil

2½ Tbsp tahini

1½ Tbsp soy sauce

1 Tbsp honey

Juice of 1 lemon

½ tsp kosher salt

In a blender or food processor, combine all ingredients and blend until smooth. Store in an airtight container in the fridge for up to 5 days.

CAESAR SALAD DRESSING

MAKES ABOUT 2½ CUPS

2 Tbsp freshly squeezed lemon juice

3 Tbsp sherry vinegar

2 Tbsp grainy Dijon mustard

2 tsp Worcestershire sauce

1½ tsp Tabasco sauce

3 egg yolks

⅓ cup grated Parmigiano-Reggiano

2 tsp chopped thyme

½ tsp kosher salt

½ tsp black pepper

1 cup olive oil

¼ cup vegetable oil

In a blender or food processor, combine all ingredients except for the oils. Blend until smooth. While the blender runs, drip the oil in a slow but steady stream until an emulsion is formed. Refrigerate until ready to use, up to 1 week.

KITCHEN TIP: If your dressing splits, don't despair. Sometimes you can fix it by blending in 1 Tbsp water, but if that doesn't work, transfer the split dressing to a clean measuring cup. Clean the blender and add 2 fresh egg yolks and 1 Tbsp water in a blender. Blend on high and slowly stream in the split dressing to re-emulsify.

ROMESCO SAUCE

MAKES ABOUT 1½ CUPS

6 Tbsp olive oil

1 cup almonds, skins removed

1 large tomato, halved

One 8 oz jar piquillo peppers

6 cloves garlic

1½ Tbsp sherry vinegar

1 Tbsp smoked paprika

1 Tbsp dried chili flakes

1 tsp saffron threads

1 tsp kosher salt

In a pan, heat the olive oil, then lightly toast the almonds in the oil until golden brown. Add the tomato halves flesh side down, the piquillo peppers, and the garlic cloves. Cook everything down until the tomatoes begin to burst and release their juices. Add the remaining ingredients and cook until fragrant. Combine in a blender and pulse until it forms a coarse puree. Serve immediately with grilled vegetables, meats, or eggs, or store in an airtight container in the fridge for up to 10 days.

CHIMICHURRI

MAKES ABOUT 2 CUPS

1 shallot, minced

2 cloves garlic, grated
   or finely chopped

1 tsp kosher salt

½ cup sherry vinegar

Zest and juice of 1 lime

½ cup finely chopped cilantro

¼ cup finely chopped parsley

¼ cup finely chopped mint

¼ cup finely chopped oregano

¾ cup extra-virgin olive oil

In a medium bowl, combine the shallots and garlic. Add the salt, vinegar, and lime zest and juice, and let sit for 10 minutes. Add the herbs and toss to combine. Using a fork, slowly whisk in the olive oil until completely incorporated. Keep in the fridge for up to 3 days.

FERMENTED RED CHILIES

MAKES ABOUT ¾ CUP

10 oz long red chilies, thinly
   sliced

4 tsp kosher salt

1 tsp sugar

¼ cup cider vinegar

1 Tbsp freshly squeezed lemon
   juice

2 Tbsp olive oil

In a large mason jar, combine the chilies, salt, and sugar. Seal, then shake to coat the peppers. Store in the fridge for 7 days, turning the jar over twice. After 1 week, drain the chilies. In a food processor, gently blitz the chilies with the vinegar, and lemon juice so that they are slightly broken up and some texture remains. Return to the same jar and cover with olive oil. Keep in the fridge for up to 3 months.

PASILLA CHILI OIL

MAKES ABOUT ½ CUP

3 dried pasilla chilies, split,
   stemmed, and seeded

1 tsp kosher salt

Zest and juice of 1 lime

1 clove garlic, finely grated

⅓ cup olive oil

In a dry pan over medium heat, lightly toast the chilies until fragrant. Transfer to a spice grinder or a clean and dry coffee grinder, and grind until as fine as possible. Combine with the remaining ingredients and store in an airtight container in the fridge for up to 1 month.

FLOCK CHICKEN DRY RUB

MAKES ABOUT 1½ CUPS

6 Tbsp kosher salt

¼ cup brown sugar

¼ cup smoked paprika

2 Tbsp garlic powder

1½ Tbsp onion powder

1 Tbsp cayenne

1 Tbsp ground coriander

1 Tbsp ground fennel seeds

1 Tbsp ground mustard seeds

In a bowl, combine the salt and sugar and mix until homogeneous. Add the remaining ingredients and massage them into the sugar and salt mixture until homogeneous and fragrant. The spice rub will keep in an airtight container for up to 3 months.

TOASTED SOURDOUGH BREADCRUMBS WITH ROSEMARY & SEA SALT

MAKES ABOUT 2 CUPS

½ loaf sourdough bread

3 Tbsp olive oil

2 cloves garlic, smashed

2 sprigs rosemary, leaves picked and finely chopped

1½ tsp fine sea salt

Cut the bread into about ⅛-inch slices, or as thin as possible, then chop until coarsely diced. In a large saucepan set over medium-low heat, combine the breadcrumbs with the olive oil and garlic and cook until golden brown and crispy, about 12 minutes, stirring occasionally. You want the bread to be really dry so it has a longer shelf life. Add the rosemary and continue to cook until fragrant, about 2 minutes. Season with salt, remove the garlic, and set aside to cool completely. Store in an airtight container at room temperature for up to 3 weeks.

CASHEW DUKKAH

MAKES ABOUT 2 CUPS

¾ cup cashews

⅓ cup sunflower seeds

¼ cup coriander seeds

2 tsp cumin seeds

2 tsp fennel seeds

2 Tbsp black sesame seeds

2 Tbsp white sesame seeds

1 Tbsp sumac

1 tsp kosher salt

If your cashews are raw, toast them in a large heavy-bottomed pan until lightly golden. Then add the remaining ingredients and toast until golden and fragrant. Combine everything in a mortar and pestle or crush with the bottom of a heavy pan. Keep in an airtight container at room temperature for up to 1 month.

SWEET POTATO HUMMUS

MAKES ABOUT 2½ CUPS

½ cup tahini

⅓ cup olive oil

Juice of 2 lemons

1 cup canned chickpeas,
  rinsed and drained

1 medium sweet potato,
  baked and skin removed

1 clove garlic

2 tsp kosher salt

½ tsp smoked paprika

In a food processor or blender, combine all the ingredients, putting the liquid ingredients in first. Process until the mixture is smooth and homogeneous. Keep in the fridge for up to 4 days.

ROASTED BEET HUMMUS

MAKES ABOUT 2½ CUPS

½ cup tahini

½ cup olive oil

Juice of 2 lemons

1 cup canned chickpeas,
  rinsed and drained

2 medium beets, boiled and
  skin removed, halved

1 clove garlic

2 tsp kosher salt

In a food processor or blender, combine all the ingredients putting the liquid ingredients in first. Process until the mixture is smooth and homogeneous. Store in an airtight container in the fridge for up to 4 days.

ACKNOWLEDGMENTS

FROM CORY

I wanted to write this book because after owning and operating restaurants for the better part of my adult life, my own personal style has matured and evolved to the point where I finally think I know what I like to cook and eat (though it's still a moving target), and I wanted to put it on paper to share with others. I hope that this book inspires you, the reader, to adopt the same casual spirit that I do in the kitchen. Take these recipes as a template rather than a strict set of guidelines. Mash them up, pull inspiration from your own family recipes and eating experiences, don't worry about mistakes. Everything in this book is malleable—play with what you have on hand, feel free to interchange ingredients and techniques. Build up a mental database of what suits you and what doesn't. That's really what improvisational cooking is all about—learning work from your gut rather than a textbook. Before you know it, you'll be creating dishes that are uniquely your own.

The food that you can put out in your home kitchen can far surpass what you're served in a restaurant, and there's no reason to think otherwise. It was when I started spending more time at home, cooking for my new family, that I really embraced this. The food you cook at home can be made at your own pace, and served exactly when it's perfect. That's not always attainable in restaurants. In fact, when you order certain dishes at a restaurant, you're getting a compromised version, because a lot of it has been made in advance. There's something soulful about preparing good-quality, in-season ingredients for the people you love that only happens in your home kitchen, and it's that spark that I wanted to encapsulate here.

For me, that spark was first lit by my parents and grandparents. My paternal grandparents—the Italians—instilled that "slow food" philosophy of food in my childhood. Before I was even able to identify and appreciate it, it was already built into my worldview. Growing up in Brantford, Ontario, in the '80s and '90s, I didn't have the culinary role models that you often see in media these days, and thankfully my parents were incredibly supportive of my early endeavors, which included turning their kitchen into a catering operationin Grade 10, and at each and every point along the way after that.

Martina Sorbara, my partner in life and in babies, is an incredibly gifted artist, and that extends to the kitchen as well. I've learned as much from her as I have from some of the most celebrated kitchens that I've worked in. Thank you for giving me the time to create this, for being patient as I trashed our kitchen for a full year of testing, writing, retesting, and photographing recipes. Cooking for you and Barlow is what's at the heart of this book.

Paula Wilson has been the only photographer who I've worked with for the last 15 years. We've done restaurants, media campaigns, and now, this book. She went above and beyond to make this happen, and I'm so grateful that she was able to dedicate and gift so much of herself and her time to this project. Aubrey, her son, was also integral on shoot days by babysitting Barlow.

A big thank you to Oksana Slavutych is needed. She selflessly donated her time and countless props to the effort, as well as her keen sense of styling.

Etienne Regis, who I've worked alongside since the early Harbord Room days, was present for every shoot day, cooking with me, and sharing his vision for the book.

Yael Korngold helped me compile my recipes and ideas, and get them on to the plate. It would have been a much different book without her early help.

When it comes to getting ideas on the page, I was very lucky to have Chris Johns as a partner. He brought humor, culinary sensibility, and friendship to our project. He was also responsible for launching my career over 15 years ago, by selecting the Harbord Room as one of Canada's Best New Restaurants for *enRoute*, and getting national recognition for a small restaurant that could have easily been overlooked. It dramatically changed the trajectory of my career, and he's been someone I've looked up to professionally for a long time.

At Appetite by Random House, Kristin Cochrane, Robert McCullough, and Lindsay Paterson supported us and our ideas. Matthew Flute designed a beautiful package, and Susan Burns and Carla Kean shepherded it through to print. My editor, Zoe Maslow—thanks for saying hi to me at Langdon Hall six years ago. It was nice to meet you. The countless hours you spent shaping and molding this book will be repaid many times over in meals. Thank you.

FROM CHRIS

Thanks to everyone involved in helping get this book out into the world and for making sure it is the best possible version of itself it can be. This is my third book with the crackerjacks at Appetite by Random House and probably the one that is closest to my heart. Feeding my family and instilling a love of food and cooking in them is, for me, one of the most rewarding and pleasurable aspects of being a dad. I feel so fortunate to have partnered with my fellow dad, Cory Vitiello, for this book. I've admired his cooking for many years and can't think of anyone better suited to help inspire a generation of dads in the kitchen.

INDEX